*KAMAAINA–*A Century in Hawaii*

By WILLIAM A. SIMONDS

ILLUSTRATED BY KEICHI KIMURA

*Old-timer

THE STORY OF A GREAT BUSINESS, PUBLISHED IN HAWAII, OCTOBER 1, 1949,
ON THE ONE HUNDREDTH ANNIVERSARY OF AMERICAN FACTORS, LIMITED

Acknowledgement is made of the generous assistance of Miss Maude Jones, Archivist, Public Archives, Territory of Hawaii, and Dr. Ralph S. Kuykendall, Professor of History, University of Hawaii in reading the manuscript and contributing valuable suggestions and criticisms.

INTRODUCTION

About the time James W. Marshall, a workman at Sutter's Mill on the American River in California, was turning up the golden nuggets that brought on a great invasion of gold seekers to that area, a German sea captain and trader, H. Hackfeld, must have been turning over in his mind the plans that led to his founding on October 1, 1849, in Honolulu, the trading firm of H. Hackfeld & Company.

This firm, whose first business was mostly the sale of trade goods from Germany, prospered, and before long was expanding into other fields, principally sugar production, for which it furnished capital. As the discovery of gold in California started a great invasion of gold seekers, so the growth of the sugar industry in Hawaii similarly brought about the introduction of large numbers of laborers from the Orient to work the sugar plantations. By the time World War I arrived H. Hackfeld & Company was a flourishing enterprise that had not only prospered itself but had contributed materially to the prosperity of the Hawaiian Islands. But it was a German-owned business and was soon taken over by the Alien Property Custodian from whom, in 1918, it was purchased by a group of American citizens and reorganized as American Factors, Ltd., in which form it has continued to prosper, expand, and add to the economic well-being of the community.

The early history of the Hawaiian Islands was closely associated with that of California, after the latter's discovery of gold, so it was only natural that near San Francisco there should be established the great California & Hawaiian Refinery at Crockett to handle the bulk of the Islands' raw sugar. While the production of gold has diminished in importance in California, the production of sugar in the Islands has not only held its own but gradually expanded until it has become the principal industry of the Islands. In this expansion American Factors, Ltd. has played a very important part.

I have known Hawaii for a good many years, both in peace and war, and am proud of the many friends I have there. One of them is H. Alexander Walker, president of American Factors, Ltd. During World War II the company, led by President Walker, made its land available for military installations, loaned its equipment to help in their construction, diverted sugar land to the production of food, made available to the military government the services of its organization from its President on down, and, in short, cooperated whole-heartedly and patriotically to the fullest degree with the armed services in the conduct of the war in the Pacific.

C. W. NIMITZ
FLEET ADMIRAL, U.S.N.

PREFACE

Less than a century and three quarters have passed since the white sails of Captain Cook's ships first appeared off Diamond Head. Yet in that brief span of time a great native king united all the Hawaiian islands into one kingdom. The tabus of superstition gave way to Christianity. Democratic government and a modern economy were substituted for monarchy and feudalism, and world commerce found the gateway to a fabulous empire.

The native temples are gone now. Brightly colored markers tell of the sites of forgotten villages. Grass huts are carefully preserved as relics of an honored past. But at night the torches flare above the reefs as the fishermen still stalk their finny prey, as of old; the outrigger canoes and the surfboards ride the white breakers off Waikiki; and the haunting music of the Islands and the graceful hulas of their maidens preserve the lore of ancient Polynesia.

The windjammers and the whalers that crowded Honolulu harbor a century ago are gone. Stately liners glide in and out of the port amid the strains of "Aloha Oe," while leis of flowers drape a message of affection about the shoulders of all who come and all who must go. Between sunrise and sunset, giant airliners bridge the gap separating the Islands and the mainland of the United States. Busy streets have replaced the crooked lanes of the old town. Where pigs once roamed untended, traffic officers now regulate lanes of moving vehicles. And at Iolani Palace, formerly the seat of royalty, a legislature elected by the people, assembles to make democratic laws.

In no field is the spectacular evolution of Hawaii more apparent than in mercantile trade. The dark, smelly shops of the last century have given way to modern retail establishments offering the finest quality goods. Wide windows display creations from the smartest fashion centers. The latest contrivances of man's creative genius may be had in ample stock. Warehouses piled high with mainland goods supply the merchants through a highly-organized and efficient distribution system.

The story is more than just a record of a business enterprise which grew from the modest venture started by Captain Henry Hackfeld 100 years ago. Although the record itself is rich with romance and color, it forms an important chapter of an even more dramatic story—that of Hawaii's development.

Just as the old Hawaii has gone forever, so have the men who founded the business now known as American Factors, Ltd. With few exceptions, all of the firms of a century ago have vanished. Times and conditions have created monumental changes. The fact that a business has survived through those years of struggle and transition is eloquent testimony to the solid foundations on which it was built, and to the ability and integrity of those who have guided it to this day.

No single man or group of men can claim all the credit for that achievement, for in the course of a century the mantle of leadership is transferred from one generation to another. In the case of American Factors, Ltd., each generation has made its important contributions. And each has jealously guarded and preserved the heritage that has been handed down from the very first—that of honest merchandise and square dealing.

Although definitely Hawaiian, the story of American Factors, Ltd. is also typically American. It begins with the arrival of pioneers, who came from foreign soil to a land of opportunity. Because of their vision and perseverance, they attained affluence and played an essential part in the development of their adopted home. The founders were European but today the business is 100 per cent American.

In 1849, it occupied temporary quarters in a small store and had a staff of two, Captain Hackfeld, the proprietor, and his 16-year-old apprentice clerk, who spent his nights in the store on an improvised cot, which was hoisted out of sight during business hours. Certainly Captain Hackfeld, newly arrived from Hamburg, little dreamed that in this year of 1949 the business he started so modestly would occupy a solid block of downtown Honolulu, with two square blocks of warehouses, a 13-acre lumber yard; thriving shops and retail stores, branch offices at San Francisco, New York and Seattle; heavy interests in sugar plantations; establishments on three of the important Hawaiian islands, including lumber yards and warehouses on Kauai and Hawaii, and an affiliated company in the faraway Philippines.

CHAPTER I

When Captain Hackfeld opened his first store in Honolulu in 1849, only seventy-one years had passed since Captain James Cook discovered the Hawaiian archipelago. The discovery was accidental. Captain Cook, like Columbus, had been searching for a shorter route to the Orient, when he sighted the islands of Kauai and Oahu. This accident in 1778 marked the end of a thousand years of isolation for the Hawaiian people.

At the time of Captain Cook's arrival the population used stone-age techniques in their building, agriculture and fishing. Except for dogs and hogs, both of which were used for food, there were no domestic animals or beasts of burden in the Islands. The people were not agriculturally minded. Although their crops were planted in well-managed gardens and some of the dry lands were irrigated by an ingenious system of ditches drawing water from higher land, agriculture was not their main concern.

This is hardly surprising when one considers some of the chief geographic features of the Islands. The last livable parts of the globe to be inhabited by man, the Islands are of volcanic origin. The center of each is mountainous and much of the soil is rocky or covered with lava or ash. Of the 6,435 square miles that constitute the total area of Hawaii (almost exactly that of Connecticut plus Rhode Island), only ten per cent is arable.

The miracle is that Hawaii, thus handicapped, should have emerged with an integrated and prosperous agricultural economy in an amazingly short space of time. As one student of Hawaiian history has put it, "no other island area has sprinted from naked-primitive to streamlined-modern in so short a period." The same writer observes that although Hawaii was the last important island area to be discovered in the Pacific, it was the first to achieve modernity.

From the economic point of view, the story of its change is largely one of fur traders, sandalwood, whales, sugar, pineapples, military establishments and tourists. Politically speaking, it is a story of rival native chiefs wielding despotic power over their subjects, of unification into a single monarchy, of gradual introduction of democratic attitudes, and finally, of annexation to the United States in 1898.

Capt. James Cook's discovery of Hawaii was accidental

At the center of these changes is Hawaii's strategic position in the Pacific. "Crossroads of the Pacific" the Islands are called—and with reason. In the long voyages between the Orient and the Western World, Hawaii has served as an ideal stopping point. The first to appreciate

10

its conveniences were the fur traders, who plied their ships from the Northwest Coast (what is now British Columbia, Washington and Oregon) across the Pacific to China and other countries of the Orient. In Hawaii they could obtain whatever provisions they needed at extraordinarily low prices; they could also employ any extra help they might need for the Hawaiians were excellent seamen.

Commenting on the convenience of the Islands, one American fur trader wrote:

"What a happy discovery these Islands were! What would the American fur trade be without these to winter at and get every refreshment? A vessel going on that trade will only need sufficient provisions to carry her to these islands, where there is plenty of pork and salt to cure it, and yams as a substitute for bread."

While the fur trade put Hawaii definitely on the commercial map, it was not until the discovery of sandalwood that the Islands began to assume economic importance. There was enormous demand for it in China, where the fragrant wood was used in the manufacture of incense and fine pieces of furniture. The traders received good prices for it chiefly in the form of silks and porcelains which they sold in the United States at much profit.

To encourage the gathering of sandalwood the traders were willing to bring to Hawaii whatever the natives demanded in return. King Kamehameha the Great, who succeeded in placing all of the Islands under his rule by the end of the eighteenth century, exerted a complete monopoly on the product. After his death, his successor, Kamehameha II, shared it with his chiefs, enabling them to accumulate firearms, boats, schooners, large quantities of Chinese goods, and a fortune in foreign currency. Unfortunately, almost no effort was made to preserve the young trees or to replace those which had been cut down.

11

By 1830 the sandalwood trade had ceased to be profitable.

Once more Hawaii's strategic position in mid-Pacific helped to bolster its economy. A valuable sperm whale fishery was discovered off the coast of Japan. Midway between the southern and arctic whaling grounds, the Islands once more became a convenient place for ships to find rest, water and fresh food. Japan's refusal to admit foreigners made Hawaii almost indispensable to whalers. As early as 1824 there were 104 whalers that visited Hawaii; by 1844 their number had increased to 490.

After the decline of the sandalwood trade, the business of the Islands became mainly concerned with whaleships. A shipyard was established for repairing visiting vessels, and stores were opened to supply whalers with such goods as flour, clothing, hardware and sailcloth. Money began to replace barter in the Islands. Unlike sandalwood, which had been monopolized by the Hawaiian King and his small clique, this trade offered business opportunities to numerous individuals. It also attracted pioneers from other countries who foresaw in Hawaii a bright economic future.

Trade began to develop between Hawaii and the coast of America. Large cargoes of merchandise began to arrive from the mainland as well as Europe and China. Some of these goods were sold to whalers, some to the Island residents, and the rest were re-exported. Three years before the arrival of Captain Hackfeld, Hawaii's imports had totalled more than half a million dollars for that year alone.

The economic changes that preceded Captain Hackfeld's arrival in 1849 were accompanied by social and political changes that influenced the life of the Islands profoundly. First of these was the emergence of Hawaii as a nation with Kamehameha as its monarch. To him goes the credit for having consolidated the island group under a strong government for the first time, and for putting an end to its petty wars. Kamehameha ruled until 1819, when he died.

Under the terms of his will, his eldest son became King Kamehameha II, while Kaahumanu, his favorite queen, was made premier. Their first important act was to abolish the ancient tabu system. This took place at a great feast held in 1819, at which men and women ate together in public for the first time. The tabu institution was a system of prohibition, violations of which were considered sinful and criminal and were often punishable by death.

Since the tabu system combined political with religious elements it was often abused by the chiefs. It served, in effect, to tyrannize the people and tie them to their past. With the arrival of the foreigners and the spread of liberal ideas, the tabu system became doomed.

Famous in the annals of Hawaiian history is the story of the high chieftainess Kapiolani who, having become converted to Christianity, decided to defy the fire goddess Pele—an action which is considered one of the most courageous ever recorded in history. Accompanied by some of her followers, she journeyed to the edge of the Kilauea volcano. After eating fruits that were considered sacrificial, she addressed her followers with these words:

"Jehovah is my God. He kindled these fires"

13

"Jehovah is my God. He kindled these fires. I fear not Pele. If I perish in her anger then you may fear Pele; but if I trust in Jehovah, then you must fear and serve him alone." The fact that no harm came to her helped to shatter the power of the Hawaiian priesthood, and advanced the cause of Christianity.

The coming of American missionaries provided one of the major influences in modern Hawaiian history. They brought with them not only Bibles but also "a good supply of the common implements of husbandry—ploughs, hoes, shovels, etc., also a printing press and a font of type." Their arrival was happily timed. Having renounced their ancient gods, most Hawaiians were literally in a "religious vacuum." But their needs extended beyond religion. Diseases were ravaging entire villages. The population was declining with alarming rapidity. The white traders had brought with them certain diseases, like measles and the common cold, against which the natives had no immunity. They were fatal to thousands of Hawaiians.

From the very beginning, the missionaries taught and exemplified, by their own behavior, the advantages of virtue, industry and thrift. With the help of natives they set about building churches, schools, and more healthful homes. "They ordered villages cleaned up, prescribed remedies for the sick, and labored day and night to bring order into the lives of the Hawaiians." Through their good work they quickly gained the support and confidence of the King and his chiefs.

Seven ministers, teachers and other workers comprised the first group that arrived in 1820. By 1844, their number had grown to seventy-seven. They not only contributed to the welfare of the natives but also gave Hawaii the basis for a democratic way of life based on a system of free enterprise. They encouraged agriculture, and under their

14

auspices attempts were made to cultivate sugar cane and produce sugar. In 1838 one of the missionaries wrote his agent in Honolulu:

"The school I find destitute of books and I must as good as give books to the thousand children of Kohala. If we had a sugar mill I have no doubt we could get good pay for the books in sugar cane, a thing very abundant here. If you can procure a boiler of good size, get one and charge it to me and send it as soon as you can."

By 1823 the missionaries had learned the Hawaiian language sufficiently well to print the first hymn book and pamphlets written in that language. In their early schools, adults were more numerous than children. At first only reading and writing were taught, but gradually the curriculum was expanded to include many more subjects, including manual training and home economics.

The missionaries also played a significant part in the evolution of the Hawaiian government as a democratic force. Acting on their advice, the King of Hawaii requested the American Board of Missionaries to provide him with an adviser on governmental problems. Failing to have this request granted, the King invited the Rev. William Richards to become his government's teacher and interpreter.

Mr. Richards severed his connections with the missionaries and became the first of a series of American missionaries to advise and direct Hawaii's governmental policy. He began his new duties by delivering a series of lectures on "the science of government."

Shortly afterward, Hawaii's first "declaration of rights" was promulgated. It formed the first step toward establishing individual property rights in land. As several historians have demonstrated, the basic ideas in the document were of American origin. The very language was suggestive of the phraseology used in the Declaration of Independence.

The first constitution of Hawaii was proclaimed a year later, in 1840. It provided for a legislative body, consisting of a Council of Chiefs and chosen representatives of the people, who were to meet annually. The constitution also defined the duties of the Governors and provided for a Supreme Court.

The land reforms made effective under King Kamehameha III were among the great social changes that took place during his reign. Up until 1840 all the land of Hawaii theoretically belonged to the King. Part of it he kept for his own use; the rest he divided among his various chiefs. They, in turn, allotted their lands to others who served under them. The commoner received a small piece of land, usually as much as he could cultivate, in return for which he paid tribute (either in labor or produce) to his chief and his King.

Since the ordinary tenants did not own their properties outright, they were more or less at the mercy of their chiefs. The system also worked a hardship on foreigners who, after being given grants of land, found that they had no secure title. The agitation against this method of land distribution finally culminated in what is known as the Great Mahele (Division). It enabled the common people to own land they occupied and cultivated, and gave foreigners clear title to the lands which had been previously granted to them. In addition, a law was passed under which government lands could be sold in small lots at a low price, thus permitting the common people to purchase additional property.

These sweeping reforms, which went into effect the year before Captain Hackfeld came to Honolulu, helped drive the final nails into the coffin of Hawaiian feudalism.

CHAPTER 2

The Honolulu that greeted Captain Hackfeld and his wife was not much more than an overgrown village with narrow, unlighted streets and unpaved alleys. Shops were dark and forbidding and the streets were deep with dust. All water was pumped by hand, or by windmills from wells sunk in the coral rock. Here and there among the prevailing grass huts and adobe houses was a wooden house of two stories, which belonged to some prosperous family.

The harbor of Honolulu was small and comparatively shallow. The wharves were crude—hardly more than landing places. A slaughter house and meat market projected out over the water; opposite them was a long row of shanties that filled the air with strong odors of fish and vegetables.

Despite the unkempt appearance of the town and the harbor, trade was booming. Only a short time before the spectre of depression had hung over the Islands, caused by the decline in the number of whalers that came to Honolulu. The discovery of gold in California had suddenly saved them from that dire prospect. The varied and heavy demands of the California market were stripping every store in town, wholesale and retail, of its merchandise. Conditions were chaotic and prices fluctuated violently. Flour sold for thirty dollars a barrel!

17

As winter came, a flood of immigrants from the gold fields poured into Honolulu to bask in the Hawaiian sunshine, and the town had its first great housing shortage. The three hotels and all of its boarding houses were crowded to overflowing. Unfortunately, that winter set a new record in cloudy days and rainfall. The natives gleefully insisted that the newcomers had brought their own inclement weather with them!

The first store was a small wooden building on Queen Street

The business of H. Hackfeld opened its doors on October 1, 1849, offering its wares in a small wooden building on Queen Street, between Bethel and Nuuanu Streets. Its first advertisement appeared a few days later in the *Polynesian*. Under the general heading of "Dry Goods, Crockery, Hardware and Stationery" were listed such items as parasols, silk waistcoats, bird cages, dinner sets, iron bedsteads and window glass.

Business was brisk. An entry in Daybook No. 1, dated three days after the opening of the establishment, read:

"Give my note favor Everett & Co. for sundry articles bought at auction, at 6 months, endorsed by L. H. Anthon, for $1,943.92. Woolen stockings, finger bowls, shawls, matting, nanking, handkerchiefs, pongee, backgammon boards, china plates, 2 china couches, cigar boxes, tea caddies, 9 writing desks, camphor trunks, axes, black tea, toweling."

Before settling in Hawaii, Captain Hackfeld had been a trader on the China Coast, sailing his own vessel. He was born near Dalmenhorst in Oldenburg, Germany, in 1815. He left Hamburg on November 28, 1848, on board the 156-ton *Wilhelmine,* and began a voyage that took him around the Horn and across the Pacific to Tahiti and finally Hawaii. Accompanying him were his wife Mary, and her young brother, J. Charles Pflueger. One of the crew members was his nephew, B. F. Ehlers. The vessel, carrying cargo valued at $8,394, arrived in Honolulu on September 26, 1849.

A trader of experience, Captain Hackfeld foresaw a growing demand on the Islands for manufactured goods from Europe and America. He had the advantage of knowing where to find them and how to have them brought to Honolulu. His first establishment was shared with one C. S. Bartow. But six weeks after it opened, Bartow had moved to other quarters and Captain Hackfeld's business was occupying the entire store.

Not long afterwards he joined with two other merchants, Swan & Clifford, in a retail store, but the partnership did not last long. After it was dissolved, Hackfeld continued the business alone, moving it in 1850 to a new location on Fort Street. The "Upper Store," as it became known, offered new goods from Boston and placed special emphasis on stationery and account books in its first advertisement. The name of Nahum Mitchell appeared as manager, assisted by young Ehlers. Because of the voluminous silk gowns worn by the chieftesses who congregated there, the natives called it "Mauna Kalika" or "Mountain of Silk." In later years it became B. F. Ehlers & Company. Today it is The Liberty House.

19

They sped across the plain, forty or fifty in a group

From the first, Captain Hackfeld took an active interest in the community. When a small group of businessmen met at the store of Starkey, Janion & Co.* to found the Chamber of Commerce of Honolulu, his name was on the list of charter members. The organization served the useful purpose of providing merchants with statistics on imports and exports, arriving and departing vessels and general price information.

Vitally interested in religion, Captain Hackfeld and Mrs. Hackfeld became regular attendants at the Oahu Bethel Church, one of the first churches in Honolulu to be established for foreigners. It must have been gratifying to Captain Hackfeld to note the general progress that Christianity and education were making on the Islands. By the time he came to Honolulu nearly all of the Islanders had accepted the teachings of the Gospel. At that time there were 437 Protestant schools and 103 Roman Catholic schools in Hawaii. Some of the residents claimed that it was difficult to find a ten-year-old Hawaiian child who could not read the Bible.

Although the port was bustling with trade, Honolulu in 1849 provided ample opportunity for community recrea-

---

*Later Theo. H. Davies & Co., Ltd.

tion. On Saturday afternoons after the heat of day had passed, the men, women and children met on the plains east of town to race their horses, and display their bright draperies. The best riders were the women and girls. They sped across the plain, forty or fifty in a group, with loose, flowing drapery and their hair streaming in the wind.

Nights were blessed with almost perfect quiet. Loud noise was outlawed. The penal code prescribed that "Whoever after sunset shall by hallooing, singing in the streets, or in any other way, make any disturbance or disorderly noise, in any village, town, or part of the kingdom, without justifiable cause for so doing, shall be liable to summary arrest and imprisonment, and upon conviction, be punished by a fine not exceeding ten dollars."

Captain Hackfeld could not have selected a better time to plant the roots of his business. By 1850 the boom created by the California Gold Rush had reached sizable proportions. The historian, Sylvester K. Stevens, observes that "the demands of the whaling fleets for the products of Hawaii were nothing as compared with those of the rapidly expanding population of California. Mad with lust for gold and confronted by an undeveloped country, the newcomers could not possibly produce sufficient food to supply their needs."

In a letter dated June 18, 1850, the Rev. Richard Armstrong reported that "every bean, onion, potato, or squash we have to spare is at once snatched away to California to feed the hungry multitude there." Another observer of those times informs us that prior to the Gold Rush the Hawaiian market had been glutted with English, American and Chinese merchandise which was waiting for whalers who never came, but that "suddenly all the merchants were deeply engaged in the trans-shipment of goods to San Francisco. Clothing, shovels, pickaxes, flour, bread, boots, shoes and such articles as were suitable for a mining population were in demand." Exports from Honolulu to the Pacific Coast ports of the United States jumped from about $13,000 in 1848 to more than $25,000 in 1851.

One significant result of the boom was to increase the value of property and attract more foreigners, chiefly from California. In 1848 the foreign population numbered 600; in 1849 it had increased to 1,500. In the following year the legislature passed a law which removed the last remnants of feudal land tenure. By this Act, the right to land ownership, which previously had been limited to naturalized citizens, was extended to all foreigners.

In this atmosphere of prosperity, Captain Hackfeld's enterprise blossomed steadily. In 1853 he took into partnership his young helper, J. Charles Pflueger, who was not yet 20 years old.

The change of the business from that of an individual to that of a company was announced in an advertisement which appeared in the Honolulu newspaper of July 5, 1853:

"J. C. Pflueger has this day become a partner in my business, which will henceforth be carried on under the name of H. Hackfeld & Company, General Commission Agents and Ship Chandlers."

CHAPTER 3

In 1844 Robert C. Wyllie, who later became Hawaii's Minister of Foreign Relations, made the mournful statement that "The prosperity of these islands . . . does depend mainly upon the whale ships that annually flock to their ports. . . . Were the whale fishery to fall off . . . the Sandwich Islands would relapse to their primitive insignificance."

There was some justification for his pessimism. The whaling trade could not be expected to go on indefinitely. Mr. Wyllie and others worried about the welfare of Hawaii saw nothing that could take its place. Except for sandalwood, which had been quickly depleted, Hawaii had not yet developed an important enough export of its own with which it could obtain the increasing quantity of goods its population was requiring. By the middle of the century there had been a number of experiments in the raising of cotton, silk and tobacco but none had become profitable enough to excite much interest. Moreover, it was far easier to do business with the whalers than it was to give the soil the time and patience which extensive cultivation required.

Most persons in Hawaii in the middle of the nineteenth century overlooked the possibilities of one native resource that was to provide the Islands with their greatest boon. That resource was sugar. Its development as a profitable product took many long and discouraging years of hard

23

work, but when it finally emerged, it became the motivating force in Hawaii's economy.

Captain Cook noted that sugar cane was indigenous to Hawaii. Yet so complex were the problems of cultivating it that no extensive effort to produce sugar was made until 1835. Even as late as 1837 the total output for that year was only two tons. The first sugar-making in Hawaii is attributed to a Chinese who, arriving on a ship trading in

The first systematic sugar plantation was at Koloa

sandalwood, brought with him a vertical mill and two boilers. He set up his apparatus on the Island of Lanai, raised a small crop of cane, and made some sugar; but he soon became discouraged and returned to China. During the 1820's there were several other attempts, including that of an Italian named Lavinia who hired natives to crush the cane on poi-boards with stone beaters and boil the resulting juice in a copper kettle. But none of these ventures were commercially successful.

The actual founders of the sugar industry were three New Englanders by the names of William Ladd, William Hooper and Peter Allan Brinsmade who established the first systematic sugar plantation at Koloa, Kauai in 1835. Their lease, obtained from King Kamehameha III, was for a tract of 980 acres. It extended for fifty years at a rent of three hundred dollars per year. The lease also gave them the right to hire natives to work for them.

A small area was cleared for sugar cane, and a crude dam and sugar mill were started. The obstacles and struggles which the three partners and their families experienced during their first year were almost incredible. Jealous at seeing their lands being used by others, the local chiefs forbade the sale of all provisions to Hooper, the resident agent. There was a terrible lack of proper implements. At one time, for lack of oxen, forty native workers were hitched to a plow. Labor was hard to find and those who accepted work found it difficult to accustom themselves to the routine of steady toil.

Besides building the dam and the mill, the partners erected twenty houses, cleared and planted 25 acres of sugar cane, together with thousands of coffee trees and some taro patches. Coin was scarce, and the laborers were paid in a pasteboard scrip made by the partners. This "Kauai currency" was redeemed each Saturday at the plantation stores. The hired natives were furnished houses and food at a daily cost of one cent.

Transporting the sugar cane from the fields to the mill was one of the most serious problems. Oxen could seldom be spared from all the plowing and clearing there was to do. At one time a temporary railroad was laid down, and sampans on rollers, rigged with sails, flitted through the cane fields before the trade winds, vastly intriguing the natives.

There was no sugar produced in the first year but in the second year the partners were able to ship a quantity of sugar from the Koloa mill to Honolulu, thus marking the beginning of what was to become Hawaii's richest industry.

At the end of three years, the Koloa plantation yielded twelve tons of cane on a test acre, from which was extracted two and a half tons of salable sugar. But the hurdles of running the plantation finally proved to be too much for the Ladd enterprise and after twelve years it passed into other hands. By that time the young partners had decided that the production of sugar required operations on a larger scale than they could afford.

Not long after the Koloa plantation was started an American businessman by the name of William French tried the less ambitious scheme of buying the sugar cane from the natives and processing it through a stone mill. The historian Kuykendall reports that by 1838 there were twenty mills on the Islands that were run by animal power and two that used water power. In that year the total amount of sugar exported was about forty-four tons. In 1840 it had risen to one hundred eighty tons but it dropped back to thirty tons in the following year.

Except for the Koloa plantation, few of the sugar enterprises in those early days represented any large investment. Yet few survived. One important lesson learned from their experience was that sugar farming and sugar milling must be operated jointly. As one writer put it, "fields had no value without a mill; a mill was worthless without adjoining fields." In other words, large-scale operation, such as is possible on plantations, was essential if Hawaiian sugar was to be produced profitably and efficiently. This fact, as will be shown, had a tremendous influence in the development of Hackfeld and Company.

Among the Honolulu businessmen who came to have a high regard for Captain Hackfeld was a prominent physician, Dr. Robert W. Wood, head of the American Hospital for Seamen. Through loaning funds to Ladd and his partners, Dr. Wood became deeply involved in the Ko-

An ingenious mechanic built a centrifugal machine

loa plantation. Shortly after Captain Hackfeld came to Honolulu, Dr. Wood acquired full possession of it.

The development of the sugar industry in Hawaii owed much to his vision and enterprise. About a year after he acquired Koloa, he became associated with A. H. Spencer in a second plantation located on Maui, which they named the "East Maui" plantation. Thoroughly alive to the importance of improving the quality of their product by the use of better equipment and methods, Dr. Wood encouraged an ingenious young mechanic, David M. Weston,* to build a small centrifugal machine for separating sugar from molasses. The machine was placed in operation at East Maui and immediately proved its value. It not only shortened the time of separation from weeks to minutes but it also resulted in a vastly superior quality of sugar which could command a much higher price.

In the summer of 1853 Dr. Wood asked the new partnership of H. Hackfeld & Company to act as agents and shippers for the Koloa Plantation, and shortly afterward,

---

*Weston borrowed a few thousand dollars and launched a repair shop and flour mill under the name of the Honolulu Iron Works. It played an important part in the future development of the sugar industry.

27

for that at East Maui. Thus began the firm's long history as sugar *factors*—a new type of business created to fit the special needs of the growers.

In a country like Hawaii the factors proved to be essential to the expansion of the sugar industry. They acted as agents for the plantations, obtained the tools and supplies the plantations needed, floated loans, collected payments, and handled the sales and shipping of sugar. The plantations could not operate efficiently without them. Many of them were scattered in remote sections of the Islands, away from the commercial world. They needed agents who were centrally located and experienced in business matters, to act for them.

At first, the factors were particularly valuable in handling shipping arrangements for the plantations. In those days the crudely-processed sugar had to be shipped in barrels to markets that took weeks and months to reach. It took a sailing ship 20 days to reach California, 146 days to get to New York and 159 days to London. Moreover, sailings were irregular; the arrival and departure of ships depended on wind and tide, and the availability of their cargo space was often uncertain.

A business firm in Honolulu, such as H. Hackfeld & Co., was in a strategic position to deal with all shipping problems and also to handle the scores of other business transactions involved in running a successful plantation. Relieved of such burdensome details, the grower could concentrate on the complex technical and administrative problems of his plantation.

Since it takes sugar cane two years to grow in Hawaii, the factors were sometimes called upon to advance the grower enough money to tide him over until the next harvest. But the activities of the factors were not confined to financial and shipping matters alone. Through their connections, they procured whatever equipment the plantation needed, found workmen to hire, and even bought dress patterns for the plantation manager's wife.

A relationship of that kind called for cordiality and friendship between both parties. It could exist only as long as there was mutual faith and strict business honor. Although H. Hackfeld & Co. in later years became factors for many other plantations (purchasing, marketing and banking functions could be undertaken as easily for several as for one) the firm and its successor, American Factors, Ltd., continued to serve the Koloa Plantation until June 30, 1948, when it was combined with Grove Farm Co., Ltd.

H. Hackfeld & Co., Ltd., were among the earliest of the Hawaiian factors. As the sugar industry grew, other mercantile companies also assumed the same role. More and more it became apparent that their skills in handling the commercial affairs of a plantation were necessary to the growth of the sugar industry. Only with their close cooperation could sugar have become the lifeblood of Hawaii's economy. The fact that sugar did eventually prosper is in some measure due to Dr. Wood's wisdom in foreseeing the importance of the factor in the industry, and also to Captain Hackfeld's ability in fulfilling the demands of that pioneer role successfully.

CHAPTER 4

With business expanding, Captain Hackfeld decided to improve his sources of supply, seek new lines, and strengthen his connections. Since this required a two-year trip to Europe, he left his young partner Pflueger in complete charge. The business then consisted of two stores, the agency for the two sugar plantations, and the commercial agency of the Russian government, an excellent business connection which Dr. Wood had recently turned over to the company.

At the close of the fiscal year on June 30, 1855 the youthful manager struck off the first statement covering the business. Assets had climbed to $93,711. Liabilities were $48,059, leaving a "balance to net capital" of $45,652. The assets included a dwelling house on Fort Street valued at $3,514. The amount invested in the "Upper Store" now totaled $9,149, and the net profit of that store for the preceding two-year period was $7,765.

To house the company in more commodious quarters, Dr. Wood erected a two-story building on Queen Street, of pressed brick with granite trimmings, with a slate roof. The first day in the new home, July 9, 1856, was celebrated by the company with a public lunch attended by many citizens.

An important change had occurred in the Island monarchy the year before. King Kamehameha III died December 15, 1854, and on January 11, 1855, his adopted son and heir, Alexander Liholiho, ascended the throne as King Kamehameha IV. In the following year, the King married the lovely Emma Rooke, granddaughter of the Englishman John Young, who had been an aide to King Kamehameha I.

There were many parties for the young couple

The wedding was followed by a great ball in the palace at night, and later the royal pair made a tour of the Islands. In the days that followed there were many parties for the young couple. Most of them were given in the new Court House, the second largest building in town, located at the corner of Queen and Fort Streets.

Brightly lighted with whale oil lamps and candles, some glowing through colored, translucent paper, and adorned with beautifully arranged flowers, the hall was a brilliant spectacle. Guests alighted from their carriages and ascended the steps to bow before the raised dais where their Majesties sat. Behind them, life-sized illuminated figures formed the Hawaiian coat of arms. It was this Court House building, scene of many gay memories in the days of King Kamehameha IV and Queen Emma, which later became part of the American Factors, Ltd., establishment.

One of the first concerns of the new King and Queen was the physical welfare of the Hawaiian people. In his first message to the Legislature, the King asked its members to consider the subject of establishing public hospitals. The birth rate among the native population was low and the death rate alarmingly high. Although disease was prevalent, very little effort was made to prevent it. The measles epidemic in 1848 and the smallpox epidemic in 1853 had been fatal to thousands of Hawaiians. Government funds were not available for some time, but after a law was passed permitting establishment of a hospital, the King and Queen took it upon themselves to raise the money through their own personal efforts. Within a few weeks they succeeded in getting enough pledges to their subscription fund to build the first general hospital in the Pacific area. Started in 1860, it has been described as their Majesties' "finest monument." Among the subscribers was Captain Hackfeld.

The fifties was a significant decade of economic transition for Hawaii. These were the final big years of the whaling trade, which for more than two decades had been the backbone of Hawaii's economy. The American Civil War and the new use of petroleum in the United States brought an end to the industry. As early as 1860, observers began to point out that "the good old days" were over.

The rise of the sugar industry, coming at such a crucial time in Hawaii's economic history, seemed like an act of Providence. But the sugar industry was to experience many difficulties before it could grow out of its infancy. An issue of the *Pacific Commercial Advertiser* in 1859 published statistics showing that sugar exports had increased from 145 tons in 1855 to 913 tons for 1858. But these statistics do not tell the whole story. In the early fifties there had been a severe collapse of the industry, largely resulting from the boom proportions it had at first assumed. The number of plantations in active operation had dwindled to five—Koloa and Lihue on Kauai; East Maui and Brewer on Maui, and a fifth on Hawaii near Hilo. Too frequently, the industry was affected by events outside the Islands. During the California Gold Rush the price of sugar had risen to 18 and 20 cents a pound, but three years later it was noted that "the low price of sugar is ruining the planters, two having already failed."

Native Hawaiians had not adapted themselves to field labor, and now their number was rapidly decreasing. From a population of 130,000 in 1830, the total had fallen to 70,000. It became apparent that if the new industry was to advance, outside labor would have to be imported. The first effort in that direction was made in 1852, when recruiters from the Islands went to China and selected the hardiest from the swarms of applicants who wanted to work in Hawaii. Sponsored by the Royal Hawaiian Agricultural Society, the project resulted in the importation of about 300 Chinese.

The experiment failed to come up to expectations, though in later years China provided one of the chief sources for immigrant labor. Not until 1864 when a Bureau of Immigration was established did foreign laborers begin to arrive in Hawaii in considerable numbers. Until that time, native Hawaiians were, necessarily, the chief source of manpower in the sugar industry.

Captain Hackfeld returned from his European travels in the spring of 1857. About that time an interesting development was occurring at the Lihue plantation on Kauai—a plantation which in later years appointed H. Hackfeld & Co. as its sugar factors. After a five-year struggle against many odds, a ditch was finally dug that would bring water to its fields. It was the first sugar plantation in the Islands to use irrigation. The suggestion that water would improve the yield came from a young immigrant named Paul Isenberg, who remembered the irrigation canals of his native Germany. His idea met with much opposition but, having enlisted the support of

He remembered the canals of his native Germany

one of the owners, W. H. Rice, Isenberg was provided with enough workers to complete the job. This irrigation method proved beneficial.* In 1862 Paul Isenberg was appointed manager of the Lihue Plantation.

One of the important social events of that same year was a grand ball given by Captain and Mrs. Hackfeld in the Court House building to honor the officers of the Russian ships then in Honolulu harbor. About 500 invitations were issued.

It was also a year of nation-wide mourning. A young son born to King Kamehameha IV and Queen Emma in 1858 died in August 1862. His death was followed by the death of King Kamehameha IV on November 30, 1863 at

*In 1949, this ditch is still in use.

the age of 29. His brother, Prince Lot, ascended the throne as King Kamehameha V.

The new King was of the opinion that a strong native monarchy was the best form of government for Hawaii. He disapproved of the constitution of 1852 on the grounds that it was too far ahead of the development of the Hawaiians and the needs of the country. A forceful personality, he proclaimed a new constitution in 1864, which was a revision of the former one. It restricted voting to those who owned a certain amount of property and who, if born after 1840, could read and write. Its total effect was to increase the power of the King by giving him wider authority in government activities. Although there was considerable opposition to it, the new constitution became the fundamental law of the land for nearly a quarter of a century.

CHAPTER 5

In the same year that King Kamehameha V ascended the throne Captain Hackfeld and his wife returned to Germany. Captain Hackfeld had been advised by his physician that Mrs. Hackfeld's health required that she live in Germany permanently.

J. Charles Pflueger remained as general manager of H. Hackfeld & Co. His reputation as a sound business man had grown steadily, and more than once his counsel was sought by the King and his Minister of Finance. A man of keen judgment, especially in matters of finance, Pflueger was highly respected in the community for the fairness that characterized his business dealings and for the firmness with which he expressed his opinions.

One of the stories told about him that reflects his personality is in connection with Claus Spreckels, the great sugar man. Spreckels had called on him to discuss the water rights on the plantation at Kahului and in a blustering manner made demands which seemed outrageous. Pflueger ordered him to leave his office or be thrown out. Spreckels' retort as he left was that Pflueger would rue the day and that "grass would grow where he then stood." Spreckels was undoubtedly a great sugar man but he turned out to be a poor prophet.

To help Pflueger, Captain Hackfeld obtained the services of an expert accountant, J. Bollman, and sent him from

Germany to serve as the company's assistant manager and bookkeeper. With his assistance the company entered the sugar industry on a larger scale. By the end of 1862 its assets totaled almost $400,000. Several new names began to appear on the company's roster, among them that of J. C. Glade, whose family were neighbors of the Hackfelds in Germany.

In the meantime, sugar was becoming "king" in Hawaii's economy. Under the stimulus of the Civil War, it became the chief source of Hawaiian prosperity. Statistics printed in the *Pacific Commercial Advertiser* of March 12, 1870, clearly demonstrate the fantastic growth of the industry. From 1860 to 1864, sugar exports had climbed from about 750 tons to approximately 5,000 tons. By 1869 exports were more than 9,000 tons. Two years later it became obvious that sugar was to be the dominant product of the Islands' economy. In 1871 it represented a value of $1,250,000 out of Hawaii's total exports of $1,650,000. During this time, the United States was almost the exclusive market for the Hawaiian sugar growers, with most of their sugar going to California.

Sugar was to be the dominant product of the Islands

Yet, while sugar was definitely coming into its own, its future was by no means secure. The high American tariffs of the post-Civil War period seriously threatened the prosperity of the Hawaiian sugar planters. Hawaii began to send much of its sugar to markets such as New Zealand and Australia, in spite of the fact that a great deal of the capital invested in Hawaiian sugar was of American origin. Clearly, something had to be done to place the sugar industry on a more stable basis and make it easier to deal with the American market, which was more advantageous to Hawaii for geographic and financial reasons.

King Kamehameha V died in December 1872, ending the line founded by Kamehameha the Great. He was succeeded by Prince William C. Lunalilo, the highest surviving chief, who reigned a brief year and 25 days. Since he had not named an heir, special messengers were dispatched to all the islands, summoning the Legislative Assembly to meet in the Court House at Honolulu and choose a new ruler.

One of those summoned was Paul Isenberg, who was to play a prominent role in the career of H. Hackfeld & Co. Late at night there was a loud knock at the door of his home in Lihue. Answering it, he found standing in the dark the captain of a small schooner with instructions for him to leave at once. Dressing hastily, he rode down the dark road to Nawiliwili and set sail for Honolulu.

Two candidates were contending for the monarchy, Queen Dowager Emma and High Chief David Kalakaua. The latter rested his claim on the fact that he was descended from two high chiefs who had been associated with King Kamehameha I, and also on his marriage to the granddaughter of Kaumualii, last king of Kauai. On February 12, 1874, he was elected king by 39 votes. Only 6 votes went to Queen Emma.

A howling mob, composed of Queen Emma's partisans, surrounded the Court House during the election. As soon as the votes had been counted, they battered down the back doors, sacked the building and assaulted the representatives with clubs. Some of them they tossed out the window. Two men, C. C. Harris and S. B. Dole, held the main door against the mob for some time.

The police appeared to be in sympathy with the Queen's adherents. The volunteer guards, also sympathetic, refused to turn out. Anticipating the riot, the American minister had arranged with the commanders of two American vessels in port, the *Tuscarora* and *Portsmouth,* to send an armed force in the event of trouble. When C. R. Bishop, Minister of Foreign Affairs, applied to both the American minister and British commissioner for aid, marines were promptly landed from the American vessels. They were soon joined by men from a British corvette. These forces quickly dispersed the mob and arrested a number of the rioters. Palace, barracks, Court House, prison and other government buildings were placed under guard. On the following day, Prince Kalakaua was sworn in as King.* Queen Emma at once acknowledged the new King.

The storming of the Court House marked the end of that building as a government structure. Over strenuous objections, it was offered for sale. According to one newspaper account, the proposal "created an outburst of mistaken patriotism in the Legislature, and caused whole days to be wasted in debate." It was purchased finally by H. Hackfeld & Co., and plans were drawn for alterations to make it suitable as the headquarters for the expanding busi-

---

*Although sworn in as King on this day, Kalakaua and his Queen were not formally crowned until some years later. The ceremony was staged in 1883 at the King's behest. A royal crown was designed and adorned with jewels for the occasion. Today it is the only royal crown in the United States.

ness. Mr. Pflueger, who had retired to Bremen to assist Captain Hackfeld in the establishment of an office to promote the interests of the Island firm, returned to Honolulu in 1874, in time to effect the purchase of the building.

One result of the Bremen establishment was the placing in service of a line of packets between that port and Honolulu, which sailed under the Hawaiian flag and carried merchandise directly to the Islands. The ships bore the names of such prominent Hawaiian residents as *"R. W. Wood," "R. C. Wyllie"* and *"C. R. Bishop."* In 1875 H. Hackfeld & Co. went into the shipping business further by becoming agents for the Pacific Mail Steamship Line, which was then inaugurating regular service to Australia.

Honolulu Harbor, 1875

The first year of King Kalakaua's reign proved to be an outstanding one in the history of Hawaii. Ever since sugar had begun to emerge as Hawaii's most valuable product, there had been several attempts to obtain a reciprocity treaty from the United States. None had been successful. Convinced that such a treaty was necessary to the welfare of his country, King Kalakaua decided to visit the United States on a good-will mission. There he was received as a guest and accorded all the honors due to a ruler of a friendly, independent nation. Meanwhile his special representatives were actively at work in Washington furthering the cause of reciprocity. In spite of powerful American opposition, the treaty was concluded during Grant's administration in 1875 and made effective the following year. In Hawaii it was hailed as the most significant event in King Kalakaua's reign, for it permitted raw sugar from the Islands to enter the United States free of duty, thus laying a solid foundation for Hawaii's continuing prosperity.

The treaty had an immediate effect on the Hawaiian sugar industry. Production was doubled within four years. By 1890 it was ten times what it had been before the treaty went into effect. There were 35 plantations on the Islands in 1874; five years later there were 63.

The heavy investments in sugar that followed the enactment of the treaty strained financial credits almost to the breaking point. Charles R. Bishop performed a signal service to the industry by assuming large financial responsibility during this critical period, thus averting the danger of a crisis. The Hawaiian government also came to the rescue by loaning the industry money for a season.

At last it could be said that the sugar industry, so slow in coming out of its infancy, could now look forward to a long and full life. Finally, it had achieved a ready market in the country that was closest to Hawaii geographically and financially. The reciprocity treaty did more than assure the sugar industry of a bright future; it strengthened the political ties between the United States and Hawaii and encouraged the possibility of Annexation.

CHAPTER 6

By 1875 Honolulu had gradually changed from an over-grown village to a thriving business community with a population of nearly 15,000, one-fifth of whom were foreigners. The city now had well-defined streets and blocks. The plains east of it were dotted with residences. It could now boast of a 42-room hotel, a post office, six churches, a hospital, a substantial jail, a customs house, ten lodges, numerous stores, stone wharves, and a brass band which performed every Saturday.

One of the Honolulu stores which had prospered was that of B. F. Ehlers. It had moved into a new and larger one-story brick building just on the seaward side of the original one, and Albert Jaeger had been admitted as a partner. In November 1868 the Ehlers family sailed for Germany. August Ehlers, nephew of B. F., came over later and in time became owner of the store. In 1881 H. Hack-feld & Co. acquired half interest in it.

In Honolulu, as in Hilo and Lahaina, wooden houses were rapidly replacing grass shacks. Even in the outlying districts, natives found it much cheaper to build of lumber than to scour the distant hillsides for grass. By then, cattle and goats (introduced to the Islands by Captain Vancouver shortly after their discovery) had removed much of the long grass that had once been so prevalent. Lumber imports grew from $50,155.18 in 1873 to $248,557.23 in

1882. Among the large importers was H. Hackfeld & Co., who brought in many shiploads from the Puget Sound mills.

In 1875 the first typewriter was introduced to the Islands by Dillingham Company, founded by Benjamin Franklin Dillingham and Alfred Castle. Other notable "firsts" of that period included the construction of the first telegraph line on Maui in 1877 and the arrival of the first steam engine for the Maui railroad in 1878. In the same year was laid the cornerstone of Iolani Palace, the first building on the Islands to be lighted by electricity. King Kalakaua obtained one of Edison's early generators, introducing electric power in Hawaii several years before many of the largest cities in the United States adopted it.

Sugar was rapidly transforming Hawaii from a trading point, a sailor's stopping place, into a land of prosperous industry. On Maui, two young men who were sons of the early missionaries, S. T. Alexander and H. P. Baldwin, brought water to their lowland plantation through the Hamakua ditch, a major engineering achievement, transforming it into a lucrative operation. Irrigation helped to open up larger areas of land hitherto considered unsuitable to the cultivation of cane, and production increased accordingly.

The tremendous spurt in sugar created a serious need for more manpower. In 1882 the Planters' Labor and Supply Company* (in which J. C. Glade represented H. Hackfeld & Co., Ltd.) was organized to dedicate itself to the welfare of the sugar industry and especially to the solution of the labor problem. Although the Chinese had proved to be capable agricultural laborers, they would not stick to the land, preferring to live in the towns. In 1886 it was estimated that out of 18,000 Chinese in Hawaii, 4,500 were in Honolulu. It became evident that some other source of manpower had to be found.

---

*In 1895 it was succeeded by the Hawaiian Sugar Planters Association.

The first Japanese to come to Hawaii, 148 in all, arrived in 1868. Not until 1885 were formal arrangements made for a mass migration of them. In that year 2,000 came, and their annual total increased thereafter. The "shipped men," as they were called, were examined by Japanese officials before their departure. The Japanese consul in the Islands watched over their welfare after their arrival. Today the Hawaiian population includes more than 170,000 persons of Japanese origin or descent.

In the intervening years came the Portuguese. In the initial group, which arrived about 1877, were 180 from the Portuguese island of Madeira, which is similar to Hawaii scenically and climatically. Unlike the Chinese they brought their families with them and willingly settled down on the sugar farms. The Portuguese immigration continued until 1913. During that time, about 20,000 men, women and children, the majority of them from Madeira and the Azores, came to Hawaii. The present Portuguese population now numbers about 30,000, nearly all of whom, through birth or naturalization, are American citizens.

Another important factor in the development of sugar was the building of the Oahu Railway by B. F. Dillingham, which at first was derisively called "Dillingham's Folly."

At first derisively called "Dillingham's Folly"

44

Captain Hackfeld was said to have loaned $50,000 to enable him to import rails. It was Dillingham who envisioned the development of the unproductive lowlands into sugar-producing areas by irrigating them with well water raised to the necessary level by pumps.

An experienced sugar man—Paul Isenberg—directed the activities of H. Hackfeld & Co. during this period. A great deal had happened to him since his arrival as a young immigrant from Hanover. At first he had worked for William Harrison Rice on the Lihue plantation on Kauai. Rice's health had been failing, and Isenberg was of great assistance to him. One of the Rice daughters became his wife. After her death in 1867, Isenberg returned to Germany for a visit, and while at the Hackfeld home, met the charming and beautiful Miss Beta Glade. She became his second wife.

Besides improving and expanding the Lihue plantation, Isenberg acquired half interest in Koloa from Dr. Wood and in 1871 became its manager. His brothers, Carl and Otto, came from Germany to help him. At that time Koloa was one of the Island's most prosperous plantations, with an annual output of 400 tons. Ten years later the three brothers and George N. Wilcox and his brothers erected the Kekaha mill on Kauai, and Otto Isenberg became its general manager.

About that time Paul Isenberg accepted Captain Hackfeld's invitation to join his firm as a partner, and was appointed active head of the company. Captain Hackfeld, J. C. Pflueger and J. C. Glade became silent partners with limited liability. John F. Hackfeld, nephew of the founder, then entered the firm, as did H. F. Glade, Paul Isenberg's brother-in-law.

Isenberg was a strongly built man of impressive appearance, who was noted for his kindness and integrity

45

of character. A consistent friend of the Hawaiians, Isenberg was recognized by King Lunalilo as a friend of the throne, and commissioned a Noble of the Realm. He was decorated with the Order of Kamehameha, and represented the Island of Kauai in the Legislature.

After the company became factors for the original Koloa plantation, sugar became one of its most important interests. By 1881 it was also serving as factors for the following plantations: Kilauea, Lihue, Hanamaulu and Grove Farm on Kauai; Heeia, Waianae and Waimanalo on Oahu; Ookala on Hawaii, and Pioneer Mill, Hana, Grove Ranch, Olowalu, Kipahulu and Lilikoe on Maui. With an experienced man like Isenberg at the helm, the company was in a strategic position to serve these plantations in a profitable manner.

The year 1882 marked the beginning of an enterprise that was to play a vital role in the future development of the Islands. A young American sea captain, William Matson, saw a need for developing regular freight and passenger service between Hawaii and California. As captain of the sailing ship *Emma Claudina,* Matson brought a cargo of 300 tons to Hilo and took back coconuts, hides, some tropical fruit and sugar. Within three years the demand for sugar transport overtaxed the little ship, and she was sold, to make way for the brigantine *Lurline,* the first of three ships to bear the name of Captain Matson's daughter.

Sugar became his chief cargo from the Islands. Sailing with a northeaster in his favor, he could reach Hilo from the Golden Gate in two weeks, or even less. With the wind against him, it took three weeks, and sometimes longer. From that modest beginning eventually grew the great Matson Navigation Company, with its fleet of freighters and white luxury liners, to provide Hawaii with the most modern kind of sea transportation.

46

CHAPTER 7

In 1886, Captain Hackfeld severed all connections with the company he had founded. A new generation of men directed the business, now capitalized at $625,000.

Four newcomers destined to rise high in the organization had now joined it: F. Klamp, J. F. Humburg, W. Pfotenhauer and J. F. C. Hagens. Young Humburg, who became manager of the Merchandising Department when he was only nineteen years old, served as office boy during his first six months with the company. A small cubby hole, where he could sleep at night, was built for him on the second floor of the Old Court House building. "It was not very grand," he recalls, "but to a boy just past 15, it was quite satisfactory."

By that time the company had acquired larger facilities. A brick warehouse was erected on Halekauwila Street (Warehouse No. 1) in 1883. A few years later it was connected with the Court House building by a roofed-over passage which was used as a packing room. Other buildings soon followed, including one which was used as a warehouse for coffee.

On a quiet Sunday afternoon in April 1886, fire broke out in a Chinese neighborhood in Honolulu and before it had run its course, the entire district between Beretania and King Streets, as far as the Nuuanu stream, was a mass of smoking embers. The heaviest insurance loss paid as a

47

result of the fire fell upon the Trans-Atlantic Company, which was represented by H. Hackfeld & Co. Payments totalled $62,250. Out of the conflagration developed the idea of organizing a Honolulu Board of Underwriters. Along with Hackfeld, the signers of the Board's first by-laws were Bishop & Co., Castle & Cooke, and Theo. H. Davies.

Neither J. Charles Pflueger nor Captain Hackfeld lived to see the fortieth anniversary of the business they had built. Pflueger, who at the time was the Hawaiian Consul General for Germany, died in 1883 at the age of fifty. Captain Hackfeld died in 1887, at the age of seventy-two, one year after he had retired from the company.

While the business he left behind continued to grow and prosper, a dramatic struggle was going on in Hawaii for control of the government. Ever since King Kalakaua ascended the throne, he had complained about the restrictions on his power imposed by the constitution. He favored partial restoration of personal government, including the right to dismiss his cabinet whenever he chose to do so. The conflict reached a climax in 1887 when a mass meeting of citizens was held to demand certain reforms from the throne. Finding himself without support, the King was compelled to sign a new constitution designed to end personal government and make his cabinet subject to the will of the Legislature. The constitution also provided that the Nobles comprising the upper house of the Legislature were to be elected by the people, rather than appointed by the sovereign.

The King's action created considerable dissatisfaction among members of his court and royal sympathizers. In the summer of 1889 Robert W. Wilcox led a group of insurgents in an insurrection against the government. They occupied the palace grounds and the government building and invited King Kalakaua to proclaim a new constitution. This he declined to do. Meanwhile, volunteer troops and citizens surrounded the insurgents. In the skirmish that followed seven of them were killed and many more wounded. Although the insurgents surrendered, the feeling of bitterness between the two parties became more intense than ever.

"During that revolution," recalls Mr. Humburg, "we had four kegs of powder on the second floor of the Court House building. I was put there to watch them. We hung blankets across the windows soaked in water, so that if shooting started we had some protection." Not long after the rebellion, H. Hackfeld & Co. celebrated its birthday. The *Advertiser* noted in its columns:

Insurgents occupied the palace grounds

"The fortieth anniversary of the firm of H. Hackfeld & Co. was held yesterday.

"At 9 a. m. the Hawaiian band played in the grounds of the office building a variety of German airs; at noon a grand lunch was given in the rooms of the office building and in the afternoon the employees enjoyed themselves away from business."

Following this occasion, H. Hackfeld & Co. ventured into a new field that was to contribute further to Hawaii's welfare. Up to this time, the use of fertilizer on the plantations of the Islands was practically unknown. The cane lands were allowed to lie fallow for short periods, but nothing was done for the soil.

The company discovered that some 790 miles northwest of Honolulu on the island of Laysan, were large deposits of rich fertilizer known as guano. H. Hackfeld & Co. and George N. Wilcox secured a lease on the island from the Hawaiian government, and workers were sent to dig out the deposits. When the first shipload of guano reached Honolulu, it was sent to Germany since no chemical establishments then existed on the Islands. Shortly thereafter it was decided to make the fertilizer available throughout the Islands.

For this purpose H. Hackfeld & Co. and Wilcox organized the Pacific Guano and Fertilizer Co. in 1893. A full-scale plant was erected in Kalihi, consisting of a three-story building for the big acid vats; a manufactory where the guano was carried through the machines, pulverized, and prepared for chemical treatment; and an engine house, containing what were said to be the largest boilers in Hawaii.

The demand proved to be greater than the supply, and the plant was soon enlarged. In its first year of operations, the new company produced 6,000 tons, all of which went to the plantations represented by H. Hackfeld & Co.

Meanwhile, the faith of the railroad builder, B. F. Dillingham, in the development of new sugar lands on Oahu bore fruit. A group of enterprising men led by him began in 1894 to investigate the possibility of growing cane on lands served by the railroad centering around Waipahu. After examining some 10,000 acres, then mostly covered by rocks, lantana and guava, they concluded that no similar area offered such potentialities, provided that water could be assured.

Experts were hired to determine the approximate cost of pumping water to a maximum of 650 feet, and engineers estimated the flow of Waipahu Springs, as well as the prospect of additional water from artesian wells, and the mountains. The soil was tested for depth and fertility. These investigations confirmed the prospects, and the Oahu Sugar Company was launched. The first sugar crop was harvested in 1899.

To head the company, the directors chose Paul Isenberg. Dillingham was first vice president, and J. F. Hackfeld treasurer. The firm of H. Hackfeld & Co. was selected to act as sugar factors for the company and its successor, American Factors, Ltd., has continued to do so to the present day.

The year 1895 saw the incorporation of another sugar firm, which had long been associated with H. Hackfeld & Co. When Capt. Hackfeld opened his original store in Honolulu, the Port of Lahaina on the Island of Maui was a great export town, and center of the whaling industry. An adventuresome Irishman named James Campbell left his ship to settle there in 1852, and ply his trade as carpenter and shipbuilder. Being thrifty, he saved his money until the decline of whaling, which reduced the number of ships calling at Lahaina during a season from 200 to 3.

This decline led the Maui pioneers to turn to sugar cane cultivation. Campbell invested his savings in a small plantation and with his partner, Harry Turton, undertook the manufacture of sugar. After numerous vicissitudes, during which Campbell sold his half interest to his partner, only to have Turton fail, Campbell bought back the property from the assignee, acting jointly with Paul Isenberg.

51

Campbell's interest subsequently was purchased by C. F. Horner, who became manager. In 1895, Horner and Isenberg incorporated the Pioneer Mill Co., Ltd., with a capital stock of $600,000. One of the first plantations to adopt the use of electricity for power, it ranks high among the leaders of Hawaiian sugar production. H. Hackfeld & Co. and its successor, American Factors, have served as its agents from the earliest days.

In 1898 a third plantation and mill, the Kekaha Sugar Company on Kauai, was incorporated largely through the efforts of H. P. Faye, Sr., who became its first manager. Paul and Otto Isenberg, George, A. S. and S. W. Wilcox, J. F. Hackfeld, F. W. Glade, F. W. Meier and E. Druse joined in the incorporation. The first actual crop, grown on a narrow strip of land irrigated by water from springs and artesian wells, yielded 7,593 tons of sugar.

From that beginning came one of the most important irrigation projects in the Islands, making possible the use of acreage on the ridges overlooking Kekaha. The Waimea Ditch, extending seven miles up the Waimea Valley, was completed and a 1,000 KW hydro-electric power plant was installed far up the canyon to boost the water into the irrigation system.

A score of years later the Kokee ditch system was added, tapping mountain streams at the 3,000-foot elevation. The largest earth dam in the Islands at the time, the Puu Lua reservoir with a 450,000,000-gallon capacity, was constructed to hold these waters. By that time the yearly crop had reached 30,000 tons. When the lower, flat swamp lands were reclaimed, this went up to 40,000.

Like the other plantations, Kekaha appointed H. Hackfeld & Co., Ltd., as its agents, and it has been served by that firm and its successor, American Factors, Ltd., down to the present time.

CHAPTER 8

Ailing in health, King Kalakaua journeyed to San Francisco in November, 1890, only to die at the Palace Hotel in that city two months later. On the day his remains were brought back to Honolulu, his sister, Princess Liliuokalani, took the oath and was proclaimed Queen. A brilliant woman, the new ruler was two years younger than the late King. She heartily concurred in his ambition to restore the ancient powers of the ruler.

It was that determination which finally brought to an issue the conflict between the court and the opposing party. Indeed, in two short years, it cost her the throne. In preparing her coup, the Queen privately directed the drafting of a new constitution, to be proclaimed on the last day of the Legislature . . . January 14, 1893.

However, things did not work out as the Queen planned. Following a succession of dramatic events, during which the members of her cabinet refused to sign the new document, the Queen dismissed the Legislature. Shortly afterward, she appeared on the upper balcony of the Palace and announced that she would nevertheless give the people a new constitution.

An informal group of business men of the opposition party had gathered in a downtown office to await results, realizing that because of their outspoken opinions, their own fate was in the balance. A Committee of Safety of thirteen members was appointed, among them Ed Suhr, of H. Hackfeld & Co. A sub-committee consisting of L. A. Thurston, W. C. Wilder and H. F. Glade was named to call on the American minister and ascertain what assistance could be expected from the U. S. Cruiser *Boston*, then in Honolulu Harbor. Thurston, Wilder and Glade went to the minister's home during the evening, and were informed that the troops would be landed if necessary to prevent the destruction of life or property of American citizens.

The following day, Sunday, saw an extension of efforts by the Committee of Safety, meeting at the home of W. R. Castle. These culminated in a decision to call a mass meeting on Monday at the old Armory "to consider the present critical situation."

Alarmed by the rising tide of discontent, members of the Cabinet met with other leading citizens and persuaded the Queen to sign a declaration, assuring the people that any changes in the constitution would only be effected under provisions of the constitution itself.

Sentiment for a Provisional Government to replace the monarchy had become so strong that business places closed their shutters, and a great assemblage of citizens gathered at the old Armory. Resolutions denouncing the Queen's actions and approving the Committee of Safety were introduced by Thurston, and seconded by Glade. These were passed unanimously. Next day the Provisional Government headed by Sanford B. Dole took over control of the Government, to exist until "terms of union with the United States of America have been negotiated and agreed upon."

At once, five commissioners from the Islands left for Washington, where a treaty of annexation was drafted and signed. Only a few weeks remained before the end of the session of Congress, when a change in administration would also take place. Unfortunately, the Senate failed to ratify before adjournment, and one of the first acts of President Cleveland, following his inauguration, was to withdraw the treaty. Instead of approving it, he sent an emissary to Honolulu to report on the situation.

On arrival in the Islands the special commissioner, Col. James H. Blount, found that the United States flag had already been hoisted over the Palace, and a provisional protectorate had been established. He ordered the flag down and told the troops to return to the cruiser. Subsequently, his report to President Cleveland convinced the latter that the revolution had been effected through the aid of American arms. All hope of immediate annexation was ended.

Judge Sanford B. Dole took office as president

Instead, the new American minister was instructed to demand the restoration of the Queen to the throne, providing she granted a full amnesty for all who had participated in the overthrow of her government. Queen Liliuokalani was reluctant to accede to this condition, but finally did so.

Despite her action and despite the demand of the United States minister, the provisional government declined to surrender its authority. Unable to effect a union with the

United States, as had been fondly hoped, the provisional government proceeded to summon a constitutional convention and laid the groundwork for a Republic of Hawaii. On July 3, 1894, the work of the convention was completed, and on the following day, the new government was proclaimed with Dole as its first president.

Among the fifteen men on his Council of State was Paul Isenberg.

Thus before it reached its fiftieth birthday, the firm of H. Hackfeld & Company had done business under three governments—the Kingdom, the Provisional Government, and now the Republic.

In the midst of these exciting and historic events, Isenberg and Hackfeld parted company with Glade, paying more than $200,000 for his third interest in the firm. Behind this change, which took place in September, 1893, was an interesting story.

While Isenberg was in Germany, Glade had become alarmed over the mounting costs of the Pepeekeo Sugar Plantation, on Hawaii, which had been acquired by the Hackfeld Company in 1890. Glade had offered to sell it to Theo. H. Davies & Company for $250,000.00. The offer had been submitted to Theo. H. Davies himself in England, and he had accepted it, subject to examination on his next visit to the Islands.

Isenberg was a close friend of Davies, but he became much incensed when he heard of the proposed sale. He arranged to return to Honolulu at the same time as Mr. Davies, and the two men visited the plantation together. By that time the crop was in excellent shape, with a fine stand of cane of a new variety just introduced in the Islands. Isenberg had known of this new variety but Glade had not. Davies immediately accepted the offer and Isenberg stood by the word of his partner, although no binding agreement had been signed. As he expressed it at the time: "A man's word is as good as his bond." In honor he could do nothing else.

However, on returning to Honolulu, he compelled his brother-in-law to resign as a partner,* and with Hackfeld, purchased outright all his shares in the firm.

Queen Liliuokalani, last ruler of the kingdom

---

*The name *"H. F. Glade"* appeared in the maritime news during October, 1901. A vessel bearing that name, owned by H. Hackfeld & Co., sailed from San Francisco with a cargo for European ports, but after dropping the tug off the Golden Gate, disappeared from sight, and was never seen again. Nothing has ever been heard of the ship or her crew, and it has been listed as one of the mysteries of the sea.

CHAPTER 9

Despite the failure of their hopes for annexation, President Dole and his associates did not give up. Neither did the royalists who still hoped for the restoration of the Queen. A cargo of arms and ammunition was brought in from San Francisco and landed at Kaalawai, east of Diamond Head. Early in January, 1895, a small army of revolutionaries met there under command of Robert Wilcox and Samuel Nowlein, in a plot to seize control of the government.

Before their scheme could get under way, an insurgent outpost fired on a squad of police which had gone to the foot of Diamond Head to search a house. C. L. Carter, who had been a leader in the movement to dethrone the Queen, was slain. Citizen guards were hastily summoned. Several shots were exchanged, and the rebels fled. After day broke a number were killed and the remainder were taken prisoner or pursued into the upper reaches of the valleys. In a few days both Nowlein and Wilcox were captured.

The government acted promptly. Queen Liliuokalani was arrested on a charge of treason, and a few days later renounced all claims to the throne. Some 190 persons were brought to trial, of whom almost half pleaded guilty. The former Queen was kept prisoner in the palace for nine months, after which she and a number of her supporters were granted conditional pardons. The remaining prisoners were also released on the following New Year's Day.

Election of McKinley to the White House brought renewed prospects of annexation. Following his inauguration, negotiations were reopened at Washington and in June, 1897, a new treaty was signed. This was ratified by the Hawaiian Senate, but did not come to a vote in the United States Senate immediately. Meanwhile, war broke out between the United States and Spain. Hastened by that event, a joint resolution approving annexation was passed by both houses of Congress on July 6, 1898, and signed on the next day by the President.

The Stars and Stripes rose gracefully

Formal transfer of sovereignty occurred at high noon on August 12. White fleecy clouds floated in the blue sky overhead, and harbor and city were gay with bunting as the populace gathered in front of the former palace. Shortly before the historic hour, a farewell salute was fired by the cannon on the grounds and by guns aboard ship. As the band played "Hawaii Ponoi," heads were bared and many eyes dimmed by tears. After a brief interval, the flag of Hawaii was slowly lowered. The band from the *USS Philadelphia* struck up "The Star-Spangled Banner," and the Stars and Stripes rose gracefully to the top of the pole.

In the subsequent ceremony, U. S. Minister Harold M. Sewall requested the officers of the Republic to continue to hold office until the final details of annexation could be completed.

Between the transfer of sovereignty and the incorporation of the territory in June, 1900, the House of Hackfeld passed its fiftieth birthday. As befitted a golden anniversary, a reception was held in the offices, on October 1, 1899, for friends of the firm. President Dole, members of his Cabinet, diplomats and consular officers and officers of the Army and Navy, attended.

Various employees received substantial tokens in accordance with length of service and position. Messrs. Isenberg and J. F. Hackfeld donated $50,000 to establish and maintain a German Lutheran Church in Honolulu. A gift of $1,000 each was made to thirteen different charitable societies, including American, German, British, Japanese, Chinese, Hawaiian, Portuguese, Catholic, Strangers, the Free Kindergarten and the Kapiolani Maternity Hospital.

The Company now was capitalized at $2,000,000, having been increased since its incorporation in 1897, by one million dollars.

Plans were announced for the erection of a new three-story and basement stone building on the vacant lot at the corner of Fort and Queen Streets. It was to stretch from Queen to Halekauwila Streets, a distance of 208 feet, and extend back on Queen Street toward the Court House entrance, a distance of 100 feet, with a like wing on Halekauwila.

Among the firms doing business in Honolulu on the occasion of the Company's fiftieth anniversary were many whose names will be recognized today. They included Henry May & Co., C. Brewer & Co., Theo. H. Davies & Co., Bergstrom Music Co., H. F. Wichman, Bank of

Hawaii, Manufacturers Shoe Co., Hawaiian Trust & Investment Co. (now the Hawaiian Trust Co.), Bishop & Co. (now the Bishop National Bank), Alexander & Baldwin, M. McInerny, Hawaiian Electric Co., Benson, Smith & Co., Castle & Cooke, Hollister Drug Co., Honolulu Iron Works, von Hamm-Young Co., City Mill Co., Metropolitan Meat Co., and B. F. Ehlers & Co. (now The Liberty House).

Following August Ehlers' return to Europe, a fire of undetermined origin broke out and practically ruined the entire stock of the Ehlers store. A new and larger building was erected on the original site, but this was found inadequate for the growing business and a third story was added. During all this time Mr. J. F. Hackfeld had been in the business as a silent partner. When the house of H. Hackfeld & Co. was incorporated, he turned his share in as an asset of the new corporation. Thus the relationship between that firm and the popular downtown retail store was re-established.

June 14, 1900, was a momentous day in the annals of the Islands. Once more dignitaries and spectators gathered on the palace grounds before a large platform erected in front of the main entrance to the Royal Palace. American and Hawaiian colors decorated the platform and draped gracefully from windows. Formalities for institution of the territorial government had been completed. The retiring president of the Republic of Hawaii, Sanford B. Dole, took his oath as the first governor of the new Territory.

CHAPTER 10

As a pioneer business man with an eye to the future, Paul Isenberg was motivated by two outstanding desires. One was to fortify Hawaii's position in the economic world. The other was to enlarge the usefulness of H. Hackfeld & Co. With these goals in mind, he preached diversification in Hawaiian agriculture and encouraged many new developments.

In the nineties he took a deep interest in an experimental farm established for the company at Kona by Franz Buchholtz. Various crops were tried out there; at one time vanilla beans showed much promise. However, nothing came of these experiments and when $50,000 had been spent on them, they were finally abandoned. The Company also attempted to promote the culture of tobacco on the island of Hawaii but again was unsuccessful. At the outbreak of the first world war it was compelled to stop all further advances to tobacco growers and surrender the collateral security it held for outstanding loans. These totaled over $250,000.

The Company's venture into coffee growing is a brighter story. The development of the industry in Hawaii, like that of sugar, owed much to the company's vision and sense of enterprise. When the firm of H. Hackfeld & Co., Ltd., was founded, coffee ranked second to sugar as an agricultural product in the Islands. Rice replaced coffee about

1862 and held that position until 1899, when coffee again, thanks to the continued interest of Isenberg and others, outranked rice. Later the rapid growth of the pineapple industry placed it above both rice and coffee, but coffee has maintained its position as Hawaii's third most valuable agricultural product.

Of the 7,000 bags of coffee shipped from the Islands in 1896, about half were from H. Hackfeld & Co. Because of the tedious care required to grow this product, it was especially adapted to small individual planters. H. Hackfeld & Co. not only gave financial aid to these small growers, but also established plants for pulping, hulling and grading the product at Hilo and Kailua on Hawaii. Additional facilities were built at Honolulu which included a new building in the middle of the Hackfeld property used for storing green coffee downstairs and for hand-picking upstairs. Roasting and packing took place in Warehouse No. 1. The company's coffee was marketed under the brand name of "H. H."

For some years the Olaa district south of Hilo had been devoted to coffee growing. In the late nineties a small group of men led by B. F. Dillingham saw the possibility there of a great sugar development. The coffee homesteads were purchased, forests were cleared, and a 60,000-ton sugar mill was erected. Steel rails bridged the eight miles between Hilo and Olaa, and the Olaa Sugar Company became a going concern. The first crop was harvested in 1902.

With the opening of the Olaa tract for settlement, Hilo business grew rapidly. A lot at the corner of Waianuenue and Front Streets and some adjoining property was purchased by Hackfeld & Co. A substantial frame building which extended over an entire block, was erected to serve as one of the company's branch stores and warehouses. Halfway to Waiakea a lumber yard was set up.

Another store was opened on the Kona coast at Kailua in a building that had once belonged to King Kalakaua. An old stone barracks served as the store's warehouse.

The nineteenth century made a ghastly exit in Hawaii. News of a bubonic plague in the Islands came on December 12, 1899. A section of Honolulu was immediately placed

Despite all precautions, the terror spread

under rigid quarantine. An embargo was imposed on vessels leaving port; schools were closed and public gatherings of all kinds prohibited. By Christmas Day four cases had been reported, and a strict military quarantine was thrown around an even larger area.

Among those who volunteered their services in fighting the plague were Paul Isenberg and J. F. Hackfeld. As the death toll mounted, it was decided to destroy all infested buildings by fire. Despite all precautions, the terror spread more widely as fresh cases developed. In firing one of the infected street blocks on Beretania Street, the flames got out of control and spread over a vast area. By nightfall of January 20, thirty-eight acres were a smouldering ruin, and some 4,500 persons were homeless.

Everything came to a standstill, while private interests were sacrificed for the common good. When, in April, the city finally emerged from its frightful experience, it was found that property valued at over a half-million dollars had been destroyed and seventy-one lives had been lost.

Despite this calamity, Honolulu was rapidly assuming the appearance of a large city. At the turn of the century its harbor often resembled a forest of sailing masts. Steamers and sailing vessels from many parts of the world (but chiefly from the United States), brought merchandise, groceries, fabrics, silks and a large variety of other goods. Vast improvements were in progress. Streets were being widened, the harbor deepened and the wharves extended. Opposite the harbor, a new wharf was built paralleling those of the railroad with funds loaned to the Government by Hackfeld & Co. Stone walls were built to confine Nuuanu Stream, and a new bridge was constructed across it at King Street.

In 1895 there were no four-story buildings in the city. Only one- or two-storied business blocks lined the streets. Then came the sudden surge skyward. "Old residents looked wonderingly up at the masons as they climbed higher and higher into the heavens." Two new four-story buildings, the Judd and the Boston, which were the first to be equipped with fire escapes, were under construction. Then came the Stangenwald building, six stories high; and the Young block, with six stories on King and Hotel Streets and four stories at the middle front on Bishop Street.

Paralleling the expansion of Honolulu's downtown district was the improvement of Waikiki, where a four-story hotel, the Moana, was under construction on the beach. It became the costliest and most elaborate structure of its kind on the Islands.

In the interests of progress, property holders in Honolulu were required to construct concrete sidewalks as far out as Thomas Square, and many streets were macadamized.

Following the plague, the main sewer system, which was then built, was extended to include the "plains" as far out as Punahou Street. Another sign of the times was the replacement of quaint mule street cars with electric cars.

Many vexing delays hampered the contractor who was erecting the new Hackfeld building. The original cost estimate of $250,045 proved far too small. When the building was finally finished early in 1902, the total cost amounted to almost twice the estimate, $482,911. Paul Isenberg was said to have advanced $200,000 from his own personal funds to hasten its completion.

A public reception and celebration marked the opening of the new structure. In the evening the building glittered with lights from basement to tower, while guests streamed through its halls. One feature that aroused great interest was the automatic telephone, connecting the main office building with the docks, warehouses and stables.

The old headquarters, the former Court House, where the historic election of King Kalakaua was held, stood directly behind the new structure on the Queen Street side. It now served partly as a warehouse, and partly as office space.

An important part of the Hackfeld office staff consisted of translators, who handled orders received from Japanese and Chinese merchants. It was their duty to rewrite the orders in English before they were entered on the books. Since practically all freight from the Orient had passed through the hands of the Hackfeld Company ever since it was first established in Hawaii, there was considerable correspondence to be handled.

Among the shipping lines for which the firm was now agent were the Pacific Mail, the American-Hawaiian, the Bremen and Liverpool, the T.K.K., and many others. In 1904 the company joined Honolulu in welcoming the Pacific Mail's giant liner *Mongolia* on her maiden voyage to Hawaii. As the stately steamship moved through the narrow channel and docked, she was greeted by a terrific din of whistles from both the harbor and the shore. A few months later the sister ship *Manchuria* arrived on her maiden voyage.

Those were the days when oil was beginning to replace coal as a fuel for the propulsion of steamships. Hackfeld raw sugar was then carried around the Horn by American-Hawaiian ships to Philadelphia, where it was unloaded for refining. Among the first oil burners in the Pacific trade, they saved time on that long trek by eliminating layovers at coaling stations en route.

Eventually, arrangements were made with the Mexican government for unloading the sugar at a port on the West Coast and transporting it by railroad across the Isthmus of Tehuantepec to the Atlantic side. This resulted in a saving of 5,000 miles. The chief disadvantage of this arrangement was that the merchandise which comprised the return cargo was often pilfered while crossing Mexico to the Pacific side.

The stately vessel moved through the narrow channel

Inland travel on the Islands remained difficult and primitive. The Hackfeld salesmen, who traversed all of them calling on merchants, got around by buggy and horseback. Their samples went along on mule back. Boat service between the Islands was infrequent and a salesman often faced a tedious layover unless he could hurry through his calls during the morning and get away before the boat that had brought him sailed. In spite of such difficulties, the company's travelers covered the Islands thoroughly, visiting the most remote sections to take orders for the variety of merchandise which Hackfeld handled.

In the same year that the Hackfeld building was completed Hawaii was brought closer to the mainland by the first cable connecting Honolulu with San Francisco. The event was celebrated on the day after New Year, 1903, when all business was suspended and there was a brilliant fireworks display at the Palace, followed by a reception and general ball honoring the officials of the cable company and the *Silvertown,* the cable ship that had brought the long line ashore. Six months later, the same cable was extended to reach the Philippines, thus placing Manila in direct touch with Honolulu as well as the American capital. Over the cable sped a message of greeting from President Theodore Roosevelt to his Philippine governor, William Howard Taft.

CHAPTER 11

The new century ushered in a new era of development in Hawaii. On April 30, 1900, Congress passed a law known as the Organic Act which, in effect, became the constitution of the Territory of Hawaii. Under the Organic Act the people of Hawaii became citizens of the United States, and the voting privilege was extended to all male citizens of twenty-one years of age who could speak, read, and write the English or Hawaiian language. Later, the 19th Amendment of the Constitution of the United States extended the same privilege to the women of Hawaii.

The first Hawaiian delegate elected to Congress was Robert W. Wilcox, leader of the insurrection of 1895. In 1902 Wilcox was replaced by the Republican Party candidate, Prince Jonah Kuhio Kalanianaole, who continued to be elected the delegate to Congress until his death in 1922.

The turn of the century saw several other developments that were to have a powerful influence on the future of the new Territory. One of these was the establishment of Pearl Harbor as a naval base. Its strategic importance had been recognized by U. S. Naval authorities as early as 1846, three years before Captain Hackfeld's arrival in Honolulu, and confirmed later in a secret inspection made by Major General J. M. Schofield in 1873. When the reciprocity treaty was renewed in 1887, the United States obtained exclusive rights to enter and develop the harbor, but nothing was done about it until the Spanish American War broke out. At that time there was a coaling station established there.

Pearl Harbor's real development by the United States Navy began in 1902, when arrangements were made for building a drydock and removing a sand bar that obstructed the mouth of the channel that led to the ocean. While the Navy was digging in, the United States Army was not far behind. Camp McKinley had been established at Kapiolani Park four days after the Stars and Stripes had been raised over the former royal palace. In 1903 steps were taken to erect a central military post on the site of Kahauiki Reservation, and two years later contracts were let for building a fort named for Major General William R. Shafter. Forts Armstrong, De Russy and Ruger followed, and in 1908 the War Department ordered a military post built on the Leilehua plains in Central Oahu. A column of cavalry moved in the following year, occupying a few hastily-erected frame buildings—the Schofield Barracks, destined to become the largest army base in the United States.

Another far-reaching development was launched when the Chamber of Commerce in Honolulu, recognizing the possibilities of the tourist industry, recommended the employment of an agent to supply visitors to Hawaii with full and accurate information. Three thousand dollars were collected for the purpose from wharfage charges, and the Legislature appropriated an additional $15,000 to give financial impetus to what was to become the Hawaii Visitors Bureau. Thus were the seeds planted for the promotion of Hawaii as a tourist haven. Today the tourist industry is the third largest in the Territory.

The early days of the new century also witnessed the emergence of the pineapple industry which, along with the sugar and the tourist trade, was to constitute a major source

of Hawaiian wealth.   Although wild pineapples had grown
on the Islands since earliest days, the first plantation was
not established until 1885.   In that year, Captain John
Kidwell, a pioneer pineapple promoter, tried to grow the
fruit on a large scale in one of the valleys near Honolulu.
In 1892, he started the first cannery in the Islands at
Waipahu.

Captain John Kidwell, pioneer pineapple promoter

The first corporate effort to raise and can pineapples
took place in 1901 when James D. Dole organized the
Hawaiian Pineapple Company, which started business with
a small cannery and a plantation of sixty acres located
at Wahiawa in central Oahu. Five years later, when business prospered, the company moved its cannery to Honolulu, to a location adjoining the new plant of the American
Can Company.   What was to become Hawaii's second
largest industry was augmented by the branching out of
two big mainland packing firms, California Packing Corporation and Libby, McNeill & Libby.

Oahu became the center of the pineapple industry, but
soon there were plantations springing up on the other
islands. In terms of Hawaiian economy, two outstanding

factors were in its favor. One was that pineapple could be grown on higher elevation since it required far less irrigation than sugar. The other was that it put to profitable use land which was not suitable for sugar cane.

As in the case of sugar, pineapple growing and canning required large-scale operations. The factors found new opportunities to be useful to this promising industry. Among the companies so served was Hawaiian Canneries Co., Ltd. at Kapaa, Kauai, represented by American Factors, Ltd.

The rapid growth of the sugar industry and the establishment of pineapple plantations created a new demand for laborers. Up until 1908 Japanese workers had been imported in increasing numbers but their immigration declined sharply with the "gentlemen's agreement" of 1908 which restricted Japanese immigration. A new source of labor supply had to be found. This time the sugar growers looked to the Philippine government for their immigration, established an office in Manila and began their recruiting efforts. By 1910 there were 2,361 Filipinos in Hawaii, a number which was to mount steadily through the years. While many of the laborers were employed by sugar growers, a large number found work on pineapple plantations.

Education in Hawaii had made great strides since the arrival of the missionaries. Although complicated by the fact that the children of immigrants spoke several different languages, both public and private schools continued to improve and to contribute to the amalgamation of the different language groups in the Islands. A high point in Hawaii's educational program was reached in 1907 with the establishment of the College of Hawaii, offering instruction in agriculture and mechanical art. What was destined to become a great center of learning in the mid-Pacific opened its doors with a faculty of only two. Although many serious problems had to be overcome before it attained its present prestige, even in its early days it gave promise of becoming an inspiring center for the development of Americanism.

Sugar continued to be one of H. Hackfeld & Co.'s most profitable fields. On October 1, 1902, the capital of the company was increased to $3,000,000. The principal stockholders were Paul Isenberg and J. F. Hackfeld. In 1881, when these men entered the firm, its capital had been $400,000. In that year the company had shipped a total of 10,382 tons of sugar. In 1902, the company shipped 70,223 tons, one-fifth of all that was exported from the Islands.*

In January, 1903, the death of Paul Isenberg came as a great shock to Honolulu. Nearly all business houses in the city shut down in his memory, and flags on the government buildings and on ships in harbor flew at half mast. As one who was beloved for his good deeds and his efforts to further the welfare of the Islands, he was mourned throughout the Territory.

The death of Paul Isenberg came as a great shock

---

*In 1948, the total shipped by American Factors, Ltd. had risen to one-third of Island sugar exports.

CHAPTER 12

When World War I broke out, the firm of H. Hackfeld & Co. was 65 years old. Down through the decades it had grown from a tiny store to one of the leading businesses in Hawaii. Thanks to men like J. C. Pflueger and Paul Isenberg, it had established an enviable reputation for integrity, progressiveness, and community upbuilding.

However, as American sympathies for the Allied Powers turned into actual participation, and the United States joined forces with Great Britain, France, and the others, it was inevitable that all connection between the firm and its German antecedents be severed irrevocably.

The president of the firm, John F. Hackfeld, was in Germany for his wife's health, and he had no personal participation in what followed. Three vice presidents directed the business: George Rodiek, who was also German consul; J. F. Humburg, San Francisco manager, and J. F. Carl Hagens, a relative of the Hackfelds. The last-named had rejoined the company in 1913, having previously been employed by the fertilizer company.

When it became certain that all vestiges of German control must be removed, Hagens and Humburg, representing Hackfeld, offered to sell the Hackfeld stock to a syndicate of Hawaiian business men, headed by Walter F. Dillingham. The latter was son of Benjamin Franklin Dillingham and had succeeded his father as head of the Oahu

74

Railway and Land Company. A price of $180 per share was determined by capitalizing the average earnings over a period of years. New officers and directors were elected, and some department heads were removed.

This took place in January, 1918. Dillingham, F. J. Lowrey, A. J. Campbell, G. P. Wilcox, and Henry L. Scott formed an operating committee to direct the business. Among the important changes was the appointment of F. H. Lindemann, head of the Hackfeld dry goods department, to manage the B. F. Ehlers store.

Up to that time, the Alien Property Custodian had not yet reached Hawaii. Shortly after the reorganization meeting, the Custodian's Hawaiian representative, Mr. R. H. Trent of the Trent Trust Company, seized the so-called "enemy" interests in H. Hackfeld & Co. These included the stock owned by the Isenberg heirs, all of whom were then resident in Germany. The Custodian also ordered that the reorganization be "unscrambled," and the Hackfeld stock returned to J. F. Hackfeld, Ltd. R. A. Cooke, F. C. Atherton, and R. H. Trent were named president, secretary, and treasurer, respectively of J. F. Hackfeld, Ltd., and the sale of 11,000 shares of stock to the syndicate was canceled.

Under the direction of the Custodian, a special stockholders' meeting was called, at which the entire board of directors as then constituted resigned. A new election was held at which George Sherman was named president; R. A. Cooke, F. J. Lowrey, and C. R. Hemenway, vice presidents; R. H. Trent, treasurer; F. C. Atherton, secretary; and Walter F. Dillingham, A. W. T. Bottomley, and G. P. Wilcox, directors.

The stockholders unanimously accepted the price set by the Custodian, $7,500,000.00, as the value of their holdings, and the new company was incorporated.

Thus was born American Factors, Ltd. It was capitalized at 50,000 shares, par value $100.00. The board of directors was headed by Sherman, as chairman, with Cooke, Trent, Bottomley, Lowrey, R. C. Walker, Atherton, Hemenway, Dillingham, Wilcox, and Norman Watkins.

Officers and executive staff were: President and general manager A. W. T. Bottomley; Vice Presidents, R. A. Cooke, C. R. Hemenway; Treasurer and Assistant Manager, R. C. Walker; Secretary and Assistant Manager, G. P. Wilcox; Manager of Merchandise Department, Norman Watkins; San Francisco office, P. A. Drew; New York office, Henry L. Scott.

Dissolution of H. Hackfeld & Co., Ltd. took place January 20, 1919, two months and 10 days after the signing of

Fort Street, looking towards King. The Liberty House

the Armistice ending the war. The firm name of B. F. Ehlers & Co. was then changed to "The Liberty House."

In his report for that year C. J. McCarthy, the sixth Governor of Hawaii wrote:

"With the rest of the United States, Hawaii has seriously felt the increased cost of living, but a policy of home production of foodstuffs begun during the war, the lessons of thrift which the war taught, and the liberal wages generally paid, and the mild climate of these Islands have tended to lessen hardships resulting therefrom."

Sugar and pineapple continued to be the main crops of the Islands. The yield of sugar for the year 1919 was estimated at 600,000 tons; that of pineapple, 5,000,000 cases. Total imports from the mainland of the United States amounted to $42,421,424. Exports totaled $88,-250,021, of which $82,409,111 went to the United States. Governor McCarthy noted that the estimated population of the Islands had increased more than 36 per cent since the Census of 1910. The total population of Hawaii was now 263,666, including that of the Army and Navy. The population of Honolulu had grown to 78,200.

Queen and Fort Streets: American Factors, Ltd.

CHAPTER 13

During World War I the Territory of Hawaii demonstrated its loyalty to the United States in many ways. Hundreds of thousands of dollars were contributed directly for relief and Red Cross work. Clothing, surgical dressings, and hospital supplies valued at more than a half million dollars were sent to war areas. In its subscriptions to Liberty Loan drives, the Territory went well above its quota. In addition, thousands of Hawaiian citizens voluntarily enlisted in the military services.

Despite the obstacles created by the war, the newly organized business of American Factors, Ltd. quickly adjusted itself to its personnel changes and forged ahead. Mr. Bottomley's first report of August 15, 1919 was a small five-page affair, but it included enough information to indicate that the company was making encouraging progress. Mr. Bottomley reported that American Factors, Ltd. had purchased the stock formerly controlled by "aliens" in the Koloa, Kekaha and Lihue plantations, and in the Pacific Guano & Fertilizer Company. These transactions amounted to $2,185,712. Loans of a million and a half dollars were made in this connection, and an issue of 10,000 additional shares to existing stockholders was arranged to pay off the loans. In his second report, Mr. Bottomley was able to say: "In my opinion, a spirit of good will and loyalty is very apparent throughout the whole of this organization."

In the year 1921 the severe depression that swept the mainland soon extended to the Islands. Revenues dropped 50 per cent, and the management of American Factors, Ltd. trimmed expenses accordingly. Sugar prices dropped unexpectedly, and new labor problems arose. A bond issue of three million dollars was floated to provide more working capital.

As business emerged from the depression, earnings improved in all the company's departments. By the end of 1923, it was acting as agent for ten sugar plantations, which produced about 30 per cent of the entire Island sugar crop.

Sugar was easily the most important branch of the company's business. Merchandising was regarded as secondary. The company became factors for the Olaa Sugar Company, Ltd., on the Island of Hawaii, which since its inception around the turn of the century, had become one of the largest operations in the industry on the Islands.

On every side, Hawaii moved forward. Old landmarks gave way before modern progress. Historic Ainahau, residence of Princess Likelike, burned, and the lovely grounds were divided into building lots. Waikiki's swamps were reclaimed through filling in and construction of a drainage canal to the open sea.

Such handsome new downtown structures as the Theo. H. Davies business block and the new home of Castle & Cooke were completed. New homes were constructed for the Bishop National Bank, the Bank of Hawaii, and the Hawaiian Electric Company. A huge triple pier with wharves 8, 9 and 10 was completed, adding enormous dock space for ocean liners. At the foot of Fort Street, the Aloha Tower rose to dominate the waterfront and serve as a welcoming beacon for travelers.

A new Royal Hawaiian Hotel, to cost $2,000,000, was under construction on the site of the old Seaside Hotel.

On July 3, 1924, the Trust Agreement between the Alien Property Custodian and the original Hackfeld stockholders came to an end. All of the outstanding stock certificates were called in, and American Factors, Ltd. stock certificates were issued to holders of record. Because of the progress it had made, the company was able to redeem $1,100,000 par value of the bonds.

During the year 1925, all eyes on mainland United States turned towards Hawaii, as Commander John Rodgers of the United States Navy attempted the first flight to the Islands. Although his plane was forced down for lack of fuel shortly before he reached his destination, a successful hop was made two years later by Lieuts. Lester J. Maitland and Albert F. Hegenberger of the Army. For the first time, Hawaii was linked to the mainland by airplane.

In 1935 came the trail-blazing China Clipper

In 1935 came the trail-blazing China Clipper, to complete the first trans-oceanic commercial flight in history, and bring the Islands within overnight flying range of the mainland, which by fastest ship was five days away.

Meanwhile, commercial air service began in the Islands. Two small 8-passenger Sikorsky Amphibians of Inter-Island Airways took off from Honolulu for Maui and Hawaii to inaugurate passenger service between the Islands and what was to become an unparalleled record for safety in aviation.

Hitherto connected by overnight steamer, the Islands were now only an hour or so apart. Before the start of airplane travel in November, 1929, they had been served for over half a century by the Inter-Island Steam Navigation Co., Ltd., and by its predecessors, the Inter-Island company and the Wilder Steamship Co., Ltd. The Island of Kauai, and Kona and Kau ports on the Island of Hawaii were reached by steamers of the former, while the Island of Maui and windward ports on the Island of Hawaii were served by the latter. In 1905, the two companies were amalgamated under the control and management of Inter-Island.

As American Factors neared the end of its first decade, Mr. Bottomley reviewed operations. He was able to report that all of the bonds had been paid off, and that since its incorporation the company had put back into the business the sum of $5,257,642.

Early 1928 marked the death of William Searby, whose work in reconstruction of the plantations and improvements in the mills and pumping plants had proved of great value. Gaylord P. Wilcox succeeded him, and H. Alexander Walker of the Hawaiian Sugar Planters' Association joined the company to take over the duties of secretary. Near the end of that year, Mr. Walker was appointed manager of the plantation department also. Three years later, he became first vice president, and Walter T. Vorfeld was named secretary.

In 1931, an important merger of plantations was accomplished on Maui, adding valuable new lands to those cultivated by the Pioneer Mill Company at Lahaina. Situated on the leeward side of the island, southeast of Pioneer, was the 3,000-ton Olowalu Plantation. Since its establishment in 1881, it had endured more than the usual share of obstacles, not being large enough to operate successfully as a

81

separate unit. After the Pioneer stockholders approved the purchase of the Olowalu lands, an extension of the railroad around the Pali for 1½ miles bridged the gap between the two plantations, and the Olowalu cane became available to the Lahaina mill.

A tragic accident in September, 1933, resulted in the death of Mr. Bottomley. An ardent yachtsman and promoter of the sport, he had sailed off port in his yacht to bid good-bye to his wife, who was aboard the *Lurline* en route to the mainland. While returning, he fell overboard, and despite the efforts of friends to save him, he did not recover consciousness.

At the time of his death he was, in addition to being head of American Factors, Ltd., president of the Bishop First National Bank. Governor Judd voiced the sentiment of the Islands when he said: "In his death, Hawaii has lost one of its best citizens."

Deprived of their leader, the Board of Directors met and elected the first vice president, H. Alexander Walker, as Mr. Bottomley's successor. Mr. Walker was a native of Honolulu, and had been educated at Punahou and Harvard. During the first World War he served in Siberia as a member of the Red Cross unit accompanying the United States Expeditionary Force, and was commissioned captain. Later in that capacity he supervised the return of invalided Czech soldiers to their home by relief ship.

To fill the vacant vice presidency, the Board of Directors transferred H. Peter Faye, assistant manager of the San Francisco office. Mr. Faye had grown up in the sugar industry on Kauai, where his father had been one of the organizers of Kekaha plantation and mill, and helped in the development of Waimea plantation. After service in World War I, Mr. Faye had joined the San Francisco office of the company.

82

In 1936, Gaylord P. Wilcox chose to retire and return to his native Island of Kauai to devote himself to his diverse personal interests. The Board of Directors elected George W. Sumner of the Bishop Trust Company as vice president. Mr. Faye was named assistant manager.

Under President Walker's direction, the merchandising side of the business began to receive new emphasis and attention. A survey of the company's activities in this field was instituted, with the object of furthering their development. It was in relation to this expansion program that William W. Monahan of San Francisco joined the organization in 1941 as vice president.

CHAPTER 14

Since the day back in 1853 when H. Hackfeld & Co. became agent for Koloa Sugar Plantation on Kauai, important and fundamental changes had taken place in the industry. From the original agency relationship, the association between grower and agent had come to embrace a multiplicity of complex functions.

In the pioneer days, the agent handled and in some cases financed the movement of the raw sugar to the market. There were no banks in the Islands and even if there had been, sugar was far too venturesome a project for them.

The plantation manager had his hands full fighting drought, pests, labor shortages, and a hundred and one other hazards that beset his operation. As the years rolled on, countless new problems presented themselves. Governments changed; techniques improved; new taxes were imposed; wars were fought; other sugar producing regions competed for a larger share of the American market; the price of sugar was controlled.

It was well nigh impossible for each plantation to staff itself adequately to combat these mounting problems. It devolved upon the agency, because of its central position, to employ expert talent and make it available to every plantation which it served, thus sharing the cost.

Freed from the multitudinous details involved in the financial structure, the plantation managers were able to serve as production managers in the field. Taxes, accounting, marketing, shipping, buying, technological research, land titles and transactions, insurance, procuring of supplies, industrial and public relations, and many more functions were performed wholly or in part for them as part of the central agency service.

Since the founding of the Hawaiian Sugar Planters' Association, two notable examples of cooperative effort had marked the development of the industry. One was the establishment of the H.S.P.A. Experiment Station at Honolulu in 1895, when Dr. Walter Maxwell was brought from Louisiana to become its first director. From that modest beginning, the station has grown into one of the most extensive of its kind in the world, and experiments have been carried on that have been of immeasurable benefit to the entire industry. These ranged from the discovery and importation of parasites for waging war on cane pests, to the development of improved varieties of cane, yielding a higher sugar content and more sugar per acre. Development of agricultural mechanization equipment and training of plantation personnel were among many other important aids to planter-members.

A second was the formation of a cooperative agency for the refining of Hawaiian raw sugar in California, at the gateway to the Mainland markets. Thirty-three plantations, including most of those served by H. Hackfeld & Co., Ltd., banded together in 1906 to establish such a refinery, and did so at Crockett, California. It became known eventually as the California & Hawaiian Sugar Refining Corporation, Ltd. Today, the cooperative processes the entire output of Hawaiian raw sugar.

There was still the problem of obtaining adequate shipping facilities between Island ports and the refinery. Believing it to be vital to Island welfare that there be a steamship

85

company whose primary interest was regular service between Hawaii and the mainland, the agencies invested in Matson Navigation Company. Thus that company was able to acquire a fleet of freighters equipped to handle raw sugar crops and to keep pace with the economic expansion of the Territory.

Just as the experiment station and the cooperative refinery benefitted the plantations in special ways, so the central agencies have served them in their own field. It was inevitable that they should play a major part, not only in the development of the industry itself, but through it, of all Island economy.

Among the agencies, American Factors, Ltd., from the very beginning assumed leadership. Its financing was credited with making it possible for some 19 plantations to start. The plantations for which the firm acts today include Grove Farm Company, Ltd., (with which Koloa Sugar Company had been merged), Lihue Plantation Co., Ltd., Kekaha Sugar Co., Ltd., Waimea Sugar Mills Co., Ltd., Pioneer Mill Co., Ltd., Oahu Sugar Co., Ltd., and Olaa Sugar Co., Ltd.

Completion of the merger of the Makee Sugar Company on Kauai with the Lihue Plantation Co., Ltd., was one of the first accomplishments of Mr. Walker's administration. Founded by Capt. James Makee in 1879 at Kapaa, the Makee Plantation had been planned originally as a home for members of a Honolulu choral society, which enjoyed the favor of King Kalakaua. After Captain Makee's death and the departure of most of the first settlers, Col. Z. S. Spalding, son-in-law of the founder, moved mill operations to Kealia.

Since before World War I, the Lihue Company had owned 51 per cent of the capital stock of Makee, the remaining 49 per cent being held by the Spalding Company.

Plantation community

The Makee plantation owed a considerable overdraft to the agency, and the stockholders were confronted with the necessity of liquidation or finding some solution to their problems. The minority stockholders were not particularly interested in continuing in the sugar business, and the way was clear for an amalgamation with a going plantation, if such could be worked out. The company had 4,598 acres in cane ready for harvest in 1934.

The merger of the company with the Lihue plantation not only joined the lands of the two, but also made possible the concentration of mill operations at Lihue. The latter mill had larger capacity, was more modern and more centrally located. The task of rebuilding and enlarging it, and removing the Makee machinery to it, all without interrupting the grinding of the 1934 harvest, was truly herculean.

The old Makee mill "train" of nine 72-inch rollers was

set up beside the Lihue "train" of twelve 78-inch rollers, giving the enlarged 85,000-ton mill a capacity of 150 tons of cane per hour and making it one of the largest sugar mills in Hawaii. The honor of starting operations in it on January 8, 1934, was given to Mrs. Dora R. Isenberg, daughter of Paul who had played such an important role in the early development of the plantation. In the next year after the two plantations were joined, the tonnage produced at the Lihue mill increased from 54,081 tons to 76,331.

More recently, another merger of magnitude greatly enhanced the position of the Oahu Sugar Co., Ltd., likewise served by American Factors, Ltd. Like Oahu, the Honolulu Plantation Company, Ltd., centering at Aiea, bordered the United States military installations at Pearl Harbor, and had surrendered valuable cane land to the government. The end of the war found much of this land irrevocably lost.

Here was an opportunity to combine the remaining lands with those of the Oahu plantations and concentrate the milling operations for both plantations at Waipahu. The Honolulu Plantation Company also owned a sugar refinery at Aiea, the only one in the Islands.

Since it was desirable from a public standpoint that this refinery be maintained in operation, it was only proper that it should be taken over by the plantation-owned California and Hawaii Sugar Refining Corporation. Accordingly, a deal was consummated in December 1946 by which that cooperative purchased the plant.

The cane lands were bought by the Oahu Sugar Company, Ltd. The latter purchase made that company the second largest plantation in the Territory.

CHAPTER 15

During the summer and fall of 1941, as relations between Japan and the United States neared the breaking point, the people of Hawaii began preparations to deal with whatever emergency might arise. A Major Disaster Council was organized, first aid stations were designated, units trained to man them, a home guard known as Provisional Police was set up by Oahu sugar plantations, a corps of truck drivers from American Factors and other companies were trained as ambulance drivers, and many similar steps were taken, although immediate danger to the Islands seemed remote.

When Japan made its sneak attack on Pearl Harbor on the morning of Sunday, December 7, Hawaii found itself, alone of all America, in the combat zone. The response of the population, as soon as full realization dawned of what had happened, was both instantaneous and Territory-wide. Within 25 minutes after the "blitz," the Office of the Emergency Medical and Ambulance Committee was manned. Less than 15 minutes later the trained truck drivers were on their way to the Armory to pick up casualty frames for ambulance service. When Colonel King asked that they be sent to carry the wounded from Hickam Field to Tripler Hospital, 45 drivers and trucks responded.

Request for additional doctors and nurses reached Queen's Hospital, where a post-graduate lecture on wound surgery was in progress. Twenty-six doctors and 20 nurses left at once. The blood bank that Dr. F. J. Pinkerton and his committee had already set up in anticipation of an emergency was soon exhausted, and a call for more brought 50 donors an hour for 10 hours a day over a period of 14 days to build up a tremendous bank.

Side by side with the men, the women worked. As volunteers for the first aid stations, nurses' aids, Grey Ladies, motor corps girls, Women's Air Raid Defense and O.C.D. workers, U.S.O. committees, and in making surgical dressings and bandages they toiled long hours. In many different ways, they contributed a large share to civilian efforts.

War meant that the entire economy of the Islands had to be instantly altered. Martial law was declared. Nightly blackouts were enforced immediately, not just token blackouts but rigid and complete even to headlamps of automobiles. A curfew was instituted, and those outside their homes after it was sounded, except on official business, were subject to challenge and arrest. Requirements of the Armed Forces became the prime consideration.

Several months before the "blitz," emergency supplies had been brought in and stored by the drug, dry goods and other departments of American Factors. They proved a Godsend when the attack finally came.

Before 9 o'clock on that fateful Sunday morning, members of the organization were already hurrying to the downtown building. All telephone lines were connected to the grocery department of the first floor, which became "headquarters." Truck after truck from Tripler Hospital backed up to the front of the building to take on medical supplies which included everything from anesthetics to antitoxins. The entire stock of drugs was completely cleaned out.

By special order of the military, a bomber was loaded on the East Coast with replacement supplies for American

Factors, and flown across to Honolulu, reaching the Islands four days after the attack. This was done to protect the civilian population if further emergencies arose. With our military defenses shattered, there was a firm and warranted conviction that the Japanese would return and land troops.

Sugar goes to war: Waipahu, Oahu, 1942

Ten truckloads of blankets—4,000—were loaded and hauled away to provide bedding for refugees and wounded. Many civilians volunteered their services during the emergency. They slept on desks or improvised cots, and answered telephone calls night and day. One of the calls best remembered came at 2 a.m. from an Army colonel. He wanted one ton of yellow laundry soap—which American Factors had and did deliver.

To a wholesale importing and distributing firm such as American Factors, Ltd., the declaration of war meant far-reaching adjustments in planning and operations, both in merchandise and on the plantations. Much of the program for developing merchandise activities that had been planned had to be deferred. For the remainder of the war, the company's principal function became the procurement and distribution of basic items essential to the life of the Territory.

All wholesale and retail stores in Honolulu were closed

down by the military government directly after the "blitz" to permit the taking of an over-all inventory listing available goods and supplies in the city. To direct this job a man was needed who was thoroughly experienced in merchandise and distribution. The authorities chose Percy A. Swift, who had just retired after many years as head of the American Factors Merchandise Department.

As soon as the stores were permitted to reopen, the onrush to replenish stocks began. Trucks of customers of American Factors lined up at the new Atkinson Park warehouse, to which distribution had been assigned because of greater loading facilities and larger space. Part of this warehouse was still under construction and was immediately completed under military priority. Congestion became so great that gates had to be locked at both ends. When a loaded truck was released at one end, an empty one was admitted at the other. At nightfall, numbers were issued to the drivers remaining outside in line, to protect their earned priorities on the next morning.

Every effort was made to distribute supplies fairly, according to size of store and inventory on hand. At no time did food run out. "We were always out of something or other," said one of those who worked on the food allocation, "but we never were out of everything all at the same time."

Right after the "blitz" a twenty-four hour watch was maintained at the warehouse to care for military emergency orders and supply food for refugees quartered at schools.

As soon as government agencies could arrange it, convoys began to arrive, bringing fresh stocks for Hawaii. Residents of the Islands will long remember the welcome spectacle as the line of a dozen or so merchant ships, escorted by the Navy, rounded Diamond Head and landed in the harbor.

Hawaii was not rationed like the mainland by use of coupon books, but it was rationed in another way, by availability of shipping space and amount of food allocated. When the vital office of Food Control was set up at the Palace, H. A. Walker was asked to take charge. To this office came monthly reports from all wholesale firms, giving inventories of stocks on hand. From this the Island requirements were estimated and cargo space on the incoming ships was allocated. The fact that throughout the entire war Hawaii was not rationed like mainland communities speaks volumes for the fairness and efficiency with which this phase of the war effort was conducted.

Immediately after the attack, all stocks of supplies and materials were "frozen" and made subject to the needs of the U. S. Engineers, headquartered at Punahou School. The requirements of the military came first. Then a system of priorities was set up, through which supplies that were distributed from existing stocks could be replaced from the mainland.

The office of Food Control and that of Material and Supplies were joined together at Iolani Palace with Mr. Walker in complete charge. He continued in that capacity until the end of the war, devoting the major part of his time to this service to the country, and at the same time actively directing the affairs of American Factors.

With the restrictions on commodity shipments, fresh vegetables and meats for the Island population were another critical need. An office of Food Production was organized by the military, under Walter F. Dillingham, a director of American Factors. Truck gardens sprouted everywhere, and large areas of land were devoted to the growing of staples like potatoes, while cattle, pigs and chickens replenished the fresh meat supply.

At the head of the American Factors Merchandise Department was Robert E. White. Much credit was given to him for the outstanding job he performed during the long years of the war.

With shortages and allocations, emphasis had to be placed on the widest possible distribution of scarce articles. Individual purchases were limited and inadequate stocks carefully budgeted. As scarcities grew more acute and shipping difficult, maintenance of balanced stocks became impossible. Much additional time and energy were devoted to securing items to satisfy Island needs. With few exceptions, these efforts kept the community supplied with necessary items even in the darkest days.

The experience possessed by the company staff, and the connections it had built up over many years, were of invaluable aid in procuring materials, and expediting their distribution throughout the Territory. In that procurement, the services of Pierce A. Drew, manager of the San Francisco office, and Francis G. Reichling, manager of the New York office, were outstanding. The Lihue and Lahaina stores were made official distributing agencies under license as wholesalers, the former for East Kauai and the latter for West Maui. The newly completed warehouse at Hanapepe was taken over by the Army, as was the store at Kekaha.

The urgent necessity for the rapid expansion of military activities in the Islands, and the resulting shortage in labor and equipment, multiplied problems on the plantations. Lack of critical materials, difficulty in obtaining mechanical equipment, a shortage of trained mechanics, and disruption of operating schedules, made it necessary to postpone normal capital improvements and repairs.

On the day after Pearl Harbor, the annual meeting of the Hawaiian Sugar Planters' Association was scheduled to take place, with Mr. Walker in the chair as outgoing president. As the members gathered, all business except election of trustees was deferred. The following resolution was offered and carried unanimously:

"Be it resolved that in the light of the existing emergency, the Hawaiian Sugar Planters' Association does pledge its fullest cooperation to the government of the United States, and places all its facilities, services and membership at the disposal of our government."

To his successor, A. G. Budge, Mr. Walker turned over the responsibility of war-time mobilization of the industry. Lands, men, equipment and supplies were made available as needed. Sugar cultivation and milling were relegated to second place while the emergency lasted, and needs of the military came first.

On the plantations, sugar workers volunteered for military training, which was carried on after hours and on Sundays. A home army of 15,000 trained men was created which could be placed in the field immediately in case of attack. Meanwhile, men left plantations and mills for military service or war work, so that within two years the labor force on the plantations dropped considerably.

Black-outs and curfews made night operations of the mills most difficult. Many of them were located beside the ocean, offering excellent targets for raiding enemy submarines, should any appear.

Immediately after the attack, the Navy closed all ports on each island except the safest, forcing the mills to truck their sugar to the open port. Trucks were in short supply, gasoline scarce, and night driving hazardous because of the complete black-out. While these difficulties threw a heavy additional expense on the industry, they were met and overcome.

In his report on "Sugar and Its Wartime Controls," Earl B. Wilson, director of the sugar division of the Commodity Credit Corporation, Department of Agriculture, and now president of the California and Hawaiian Sugar Refining Corporation, Ltd., paid this tribute to the Hawaiian growers: "The versatility and adaptability of the sugar industry of the Hawaiian Islands in meeting these new conditions make their record outstanding in sugar production during the war."

After the first shock of the war had passed and critical needs had been met, sugar production and that of the by-product molasses became of utmost importance. The military extended full cooperation to the industry, making shipping bottoms available in holds that had brought war cargoes, and supply tankers for the movement of molasses, valuable in munitions.

While all plantations cooperated in the war effort, the Oahu Sugar Company, Ltd., stretching from the mountains to the shores of Pearl Harbor, and adjacent Honolulu Plantation Company, felt the full brunt of the sneak attack on Sunday morning, December 7. It took place literally in Oahu's "front yard." Japanese warplanes zoomed in with their bombs and machine guns, and not only killed and wounded civilians, but riddled the mill and damaged houses.

Every plantation felt the impact of the war in greater or less extent. Facilities and large areas of cultivated land were made available to the military. Sugar fields bristled with gun emplacements, bases, searchlight batteries, storage depots, military roads and even airports.

In some cases entire villages were moved to new locations to make way for the military machine. Skilled mechanics, drivers and other workers left the fields to serve Uncle Sam.

Great quantities of munitions were stored in dozens of huge tunnels in gulches where tall cane had previously grown. Some of the bombs that fell on Tokyo were once hidden in Waipahu gulches. Fast night fighters took off on long flights over the Pacific from airports that only recently had been cane fields.

Plantation lands along the shore were used for bases, from which went landing craft used in beachhead assaults against the westward islands. Other bases were constructed for the Seabees and the Army. Thousands of prisoners of war were confined behind barbed wire in camps and gulches. Thousands of acres were diverted to food production.

As president of H.S.P.A., to which he had been elected again in 1945, Mr. Walker reported: "The total area of cane land under cultivation was reduced during the war by slightly more than 22,000 acres."

Despite the losses in acreage, every effort was expended to produce the maximum amount of sugar, because it was on the essential list and the supply available to the United States had been drastically curtailed by submarine activity in the Caribbean. During 1943, at the height of the war, the plantations of the Territory shipped 885,000 tons of raw sugar, only 7 per cent less than the volume for the last normal pre-war year. Of that total, American Factors, Ltd., maintained its production ratio, supplying nearly one-third.

CHAPTER 16

The end of World War II found Hawaii in the midst of a period of expansion and growth which overtaxed every facility. The number of Island residents passed the half million mark. In a single year, building permits soared over 50 per cent in value. Business faced the necessity of reconverting to peacetime conditions as rapidly as possible. Many new problems presented themselves—providing jobs for returning veterans, modernizing stores and equipment, rehabilitating industry, preparing for the returning tourist trade.

Like other members of the community, American Factors, Ltd., picked up where it left off on December 7, 1941. Because it was engaged in several different fields of business activity, sugar and pineapple factors, merchandise wholesalers and retailers, and general insurance agents, it had to meet more than the usual number of problems. The depreciation of the war years on the plantations presented a formidable task of rehabilitation. This ranged from the replacement of overworked mechanical equipment to the restoration of cane fields to cultivation.

Along with this rehabilitation program was the reinstitution of the plans for merchandising expansion. These had been formulated as an outgrowth of the survey made just prior to the war. After business began to resume a normal aspect, the company was able to take up these plans once more and put them into effect.

Robert E. White, who had done such an outstanding job during the war, was made vice president in charge of wholesale operations. When he retired on August 1, 1946, M. L. Berlinger, who had succeeded Mr. Lindemann as manager of The Liberty House, was placed in charge of all merchandising, wholesale and retail, and was elected a vice president.

Adequate warehouse facilities were provided to handle the growing business. A 13-acre lumber yard with up-to-date mill was established on the outskirts of Honolulu, near the waterfront. In 1946, the lumber yard at Hilo was destroyed by tidal wave. A new yard and mill covering 7½ acres of ground and including the most modern facilities was built and opened late in 1948. On Kauai, where the American Factors wholesale operations had been carried on under the name of C. B. Hofgaard & Co., Ltd. since 1921, the operations were now streamlined by establishment of a direct branch.

New lines were acquired. The list of mainland suppliers which the firm came to represent reads like a "Who's Who" of American business. In 1948 Willard L. Doering was named manager of the wholesale division, following the untimely death of William C. Foster.

In the meantime, Sherwood M. Lowrey, who had served the organization since the time of World War I, retired as Treasurer, and Walter M. Vorfeld was elected to that office. J. E. Ednie, assistant secretary and assistant treasurer, succeeded Mr. Vorfeld as Secretary.

Pierce A. Drew, who had ably handled the company's mainland business for a period of 30 years, retired as manager of the San Francisco branch. Emmett G. Solomon, vice-president in charge of industrial relations at Honolulu, succeeded him.

Turning toward the Far East, the company reached

The company reached across the Pacific to Manila

across the Pacific and opened an office in Manila, extending its merchandising activities to the Philippine Islands.

Before the war, the expansion of the Waikiki area both as a residential section and a tourist mecca, caused The Liberty House to extend branch service there. In 1937, a store dealing in fashions and beach wear was opened opposite the Royal Hawaiian Hotel. Soon after the war, it started another shop in Kailua, on the windward side of the island, for the convenience of the many customers residing in that locality.

To meet the growing demands in Waikiki, the company began an important development in 1947. It was decided to make the entire shopping block opposite the Royal Hawaiian an American Factors operation. The drug store at one end was acquired, improved and renamed the Waikiki Pharmacy. The Liberty House at the other end began to take over the leases of all the shops in between, thereby doubling its size and providing this section with a real specialty shop catering to the needs of visitor and resident clientele.

Shortly after the close of World War I the firm acquired Henry May & Company, which had operated one of the first grocery stores in Honolulu. The brand of Kona coffee bearing the name of "Mayflower" had been pioneered by it. Grown, roasted, and ground in Hawaii, the brand attained wide popularity. After the change in ownership, the coffee packaged by American Factors was concentrated under the Mayflower label, and the most modern equipment was installed to complete the largest plant for coffee processing in the Islands.

One of the important steps in rounding out the complete merchandising program was the acquisition of W. A. Ramsay, Ltd., serving the field of industrial sales and engineering, air conditioning, commercial refrigeration and ventilation, and the finest of household appliances.

When the founder of the business decided to retire, American Factors was able to acquire a going enterprise in a field which would have taken years to develop otherwise.

Expansion of the Insurance Division was another major step in the company's progress. Originally established to insure stocks of merchandise and sugar, its service was extended to include the general public and in 1897, it was formally established as a separate department. Thus today it is more than half a century old.

When the company was reorganized in 1918, James Macconel was placed in charge. At that time, about a dozen persons were employed in the office, and the staff included three or four special agents. With the retirement of Mr. Macconel in 1946, his assistant, C. Hutton Smith, was named head.

Today the department is a full fledged division of the company, occupying an entire wing of the second floor. Some 65 employees comprise the office staff, and more than 20 special agents serve the ever increasing clientele.

Practically all forms of insurance are handled by the Division. The work is departmentalized into twelve subdivisions, including such fields as Fire, Casualty, Bonding and Burglary, Life, and Group Life and Annuity; and such helpful adjuncts as Engineering, Auditing and Safety, Accounting, Claims, Production, and Insurance Surveys.

Besides the main office at Honolulu, the Insurance Division operates a direct branch at Lihue, Kauai. It covers the islands through 14 sub-agents stationed on Hawaii, Kauai, Maui and Oahu. There is a total of 34 solicitors. The companies represented include some of the oldest and best known in the insurance field.

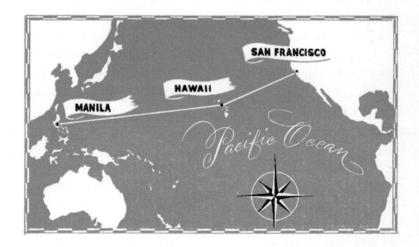

CHAPTER 17

For a century, the firm which began as H. Hackfeld & Co. and became American Factors, Ltd. has kept pace with the progress of the Islands which it serves.

Today, when the traveler reaches Hawaii, he alights from a sky giant at a world airport, steps into an automobile, and drives along a paved boulevard, directed here and there by traffic police, to draw up before a beautiful and modern hotel. Or, arriving by palatial steamship, he disembarks to find every convenience awaiting him.

Everywhere is modernity. Gone are the winding coral roadways, the oldstyle hotels with their wide lanais, the quaint wooden sheds along the waterfront, but the charm of old Hawaii—the same moonlit nights, the same nodding coconut palms, the same sun-splashed beaches and perfect climate—still remains.

The arriving traveler discovers a cosmopolitan land, populated by descendants of many races who dwell together in amity. For not quite half of the past century the islands were ruled by Polynesian monarchs; then after a brief interval they were joined to the United States as a Territory.

Conditions changed with the march of events. A throne toppled; two world wars were fought; an industrial age supplanted the taro patches and duck ponds.

Deep in the holds of huge freighters, cargoes of raw sugar, of canned pineapple and coffee cross the ocean to stock mainland stores.* Back across the water come the products of a thousand factories and mills to fill the warehouses and supply the homes of a busy, industrious people.

Business must keep up with the growing needs. Four-lane thoroughfares reach out from the city. Engineers talk of driving a tunnel through the Koolau range. Airplanes link together the necklace of Islands with over a hundred flights daily. Argosies of the sky spread their wings toward the Far East.

The arriving traveler finds a cosmopolitan land

When Captain Hackfeld set up his store back in 1849, it took months for ships to reach Hawaii from the distant principal sources of supply. Gradually that span of time was shortened to weeks, and now to five days by water, and less than ten hours by air. Passage between the Islands has been shortened to less than an hour in most cases from Honolulu to all save one of the group. Communications—once dependent on sail and steam—now flash across the ocean with the speed of a New York to Washington call.

---

*The value of Hawaiian products exported to the mainland in 1947 was $181,330,471. Sugar and molasses exports were $98,614,735. Pineapple solid pack and juice were $75,166,545. Coffee totalled $1,530,809.

Despite its great distance from the mainland, Hawaii has found in this modern age a closer bond to the mainland, and new hope for its own destiny as an integral part of the United States.

In the development of the Islands to their present high standard of civilization and economy, the older business firms of Hawaii have contributed their full share. Through the years they have repeatedly demonstrated their faith in the potentialities of Hawaii and its people. Their crusading efforts in a country that was undeveloped; their determination to overcome the serious obstacles confronting a land which for many years was handicapped by its isolation have been tremendous factors in the prosperity and welfare of Hawaii. In their constant pursuit of a progressive course of action, they have helped achieve a civilization equal to that of any other part of the United States.

American Factors is proud to be one of these firms. Like Hawaii, it too rose from humble beginnings. In 1849 when Captain Hackfeld went into business he had a small capital of a few thousand dollars, and one employee. Today American Factors employs 1,602 and has assets totalling $36,000,000. But equal in value to these assets is the good will the firm has created in Hawaii through its contribution to the development of the Islands.

Now on the threshold of its second century, American Factors, Ltd. dedicates itself to extending that good will by providing an even larger measure of service to the land and its people—and to the building of a greater, happier and more prosperous Hawaii, America's front door in the Pacific.